BRITISH RAILWAYS

PAST and PRESENT

No 33

M. P. PICKERING
23 CYMMAU LANE
ABERMORDDU
CAERGWRLE
WREXHAM, CLWYD
LL12 9DH

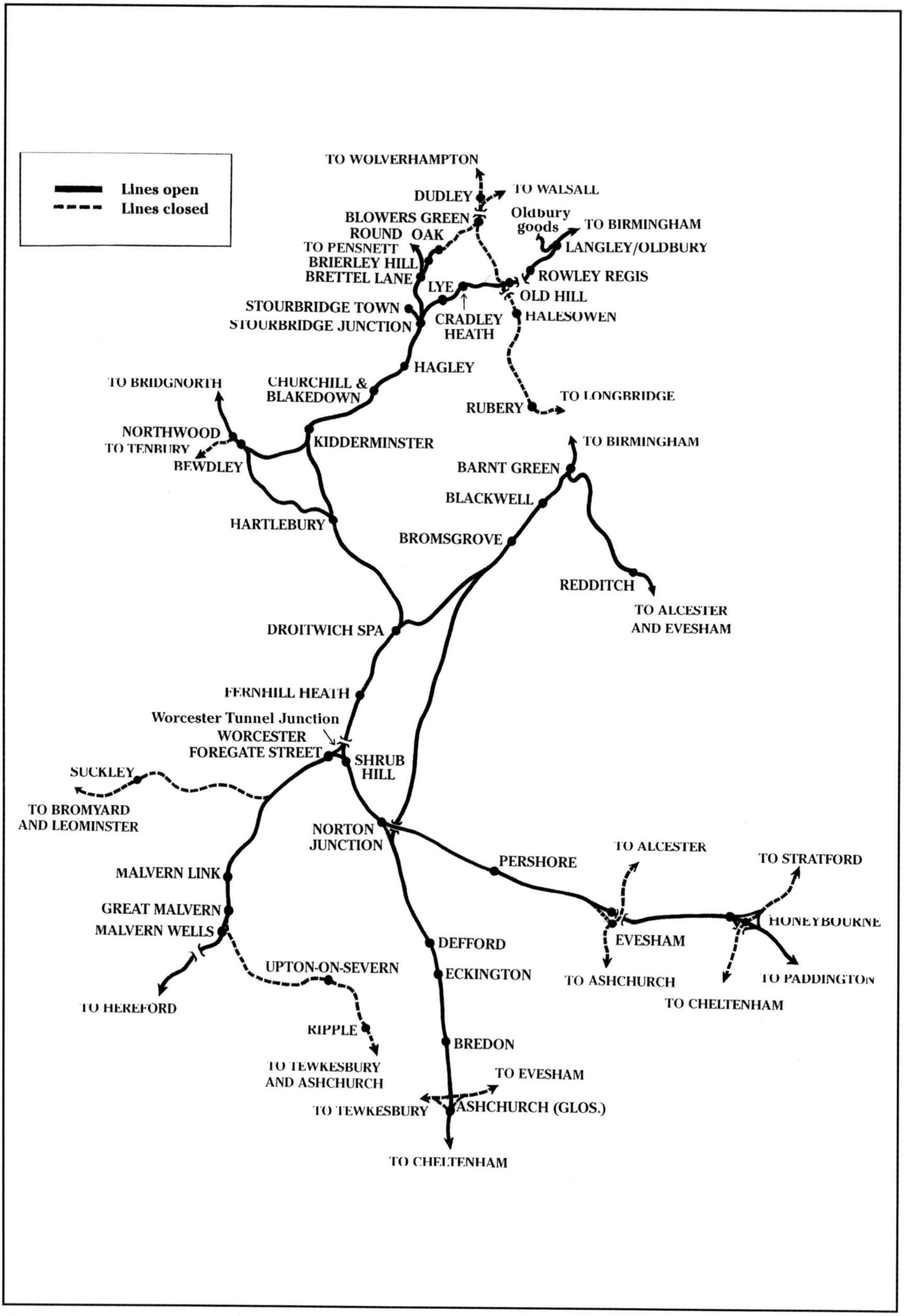

Lines open
Lines closed
TO WOLVERHAMPTON
DUDLEY
TO WALSALL
BLOWERS GREEN
Oldbury goods
TO BIRMINGHAM
ROUND OAK
TO PENSNETT
LANGLEY/OLDBURY
BRIERLEY HILL
BRETTEL LANE
ROWLEY REGIS
LYE
OLD HILL
STOURBRIDGE TOWN
STOURBRIDGE JUNCTION
CRADLEY HEATH
HALESOWEN
HAGLEY
TO BRIDGNORTH
CHURCHILL & BLAKEDOWN
TO LONGBRIDGE
RUBERY
NORTHWOOD
TO TENBURY
KIDDERMINSTER
BEWDLEY
TO BIRMINGHAM
BARNT GREEN
BLACKWELL
HARTLEBURY
BROMSGROVE
REDDITCH
TO ALCESTER AND EVESHAM
DROITWICH SPA
FERNHILL HEATH
Worcester Tunnel Junction
WORCESTER FOREGATE STREET
SHRUB HILL
SUCKLEY
TO BROMYARD AND LEOMINSTER
NORTON JUNCTION
PERSHORE
TO ALCESTER
TO STRATFORD
MALVERN LINK
GREAT MALVERN
HONEYBOURNE
MALVERN WELLS
EVESHAM
DEFFORD
UPTON-ON-SEVERN
ECKINGTON
TO ASHCHURCH
TO PADDINGTON
TO CHELTENHAM
TO HEREFORD
RIPPLE
BREDON
TO TEWKESBURY AND ASHCHURCH
TO EVESHAM
TO TEWKESBURY
ASHCHURCH (GLOS.)
TO CHELTENHAM

BRITISH RAILWAYS

PAST and PRESENT

No 33
Worcestershire

Roger Siviter ARPS

Past & Present Publishing Ltd

© Roger Siviter 1999

All rights reserved. No part of this publication may be reproduced, stored in a retrieval system or transmitted, in any form or by any means, electronic, mechanical, photocopying, recording or otherwise, without prior permission in writing from Past & Present Publishing Ltd.

First published in September 1999

British Library Cataloguing in Publication Data

A catalogue record for this book is available from the British Library.

ISBN 1 85895 161 5

Past & Present Publishing Ltd
The Trundle
Ringstead Road
Great Addington
Kettering
Northants
NN14 4BW

Tel/Fax: 01536 330588
email: salesaslinkp-p.demon.co.uk

Maps drawn by Christina Siviter

Printed and bound in Great Britain

ACKNOWLEDGEMENTS

In compiling this book I have many people to thank: all the railwaymen who make it all possible; the photographers individually credited herein; Peter Townsend and the staff at Past & Present Publishing Ltd; my wife Christina for the maps and typing, etc; and finally all the people who allowed me on to their land to take that elusive 'present' picture.

BIBLIOGRAPHY

A Regional history of the Railways of Great Britain: Volume 7, The West Midlands *by Rex Christiansen (David & Charles)*
British Railways Past and Present: No 5, The West Midlands by John Whitehouse and Geoff Dowling (Past & Present Publishing Ltd)

British Railways Past & Present Special: The Severn Valley Railway *by Roger Siviter (Past & Present Publishing Ltd)*

Railway Magazine
Railway World
Trains Illustrated

CONTENTS

Introduction	7
Western Birmingham:	
Old Hill, Halesowen and Dudley	9
Stourbridge	33
Through Kidderminster to Worcester	42
Worcester Foregate Street to Malvern and Upton	58
Worcester Shrub Hill to Evesham	
and Honeybourne	70
Down the Lickey to Bromsgrove	86
Bromsgrove to Ashchurch	106
Special trains in Worcestershire	120
Index of locations	128

LICKEY BANK: I suppose the most famous stretch of railway track in Worcestershire, and arguably in the British Isles, is the Lickey Bank – 2 miles at 1 in 37¾ from Bromsgrove in the south to Blackwell in the north. Steam had virtually finished in the area at the end of the summer timetable in 1964, so when this picture was taken on 13 May 1966 of 'Peak' Class diesel No D113 on a morning Bristol to Birmingham New Street train as it neared the summit of the climb just below Blackwell, all trains were diesel-hauled. The only times that steam was seen on the line were the very occasional light engine movements.

In the last couple of years steam has made a welcome return to the line on special charter trains. Indeed, nowadays you are more likely to see steam on the Lickey Bank than a 'Peak', which today also survive only in preservation. *Roger Siviter*

INTRODUCTION

Worcestershire for the most part is a county of considerable beauty, with rolling hillsides and the mighty River Severn running through rich farmlands. However, at one time within its northern borders were the manufacturing towns of Halesowen, Oldbury and Stourbridge, and also Dudley, which although in Worcestershire was actually an island of the county, set in Staffordshire. When the West Midlands was formed in the 1970s, the towns became part of this vast conurbation. However, for the purposes of this book these towns, which locally are always associated with Worcestershire, will rightly be included.

In pre-nationalisation days, both the Great Western Railway (GWR) and the London Midland & Scottish Railway (LMS) had main lines, secondary main lines and branch lines running through Worcestershire. The LMS Birmingham to Bristol main line, which runs from north to south through the county, boasts one of the most famous railway inclines in the world - the Lickey Bank at Bromsgrove. When steam made a welcome return to this line in November 1997, thousands made the pilgrimage to Bromsgrove (from as far afield as the United States and Japan) to see steam at work on the bank, and they were not to be disappointed, for it was a glorious sight on a glorious day.

Having been born in Stourbridge and having lived in Halesowen until I was a teenager, I spent a lot of my trainspotting days in the early post-war years on the Birmingham Snow Hill-Stourbridge Junction-Worcester secondary main line, chiefly at Stourbridge Junction station, which meant a Midland Red 130 bus ride to Stourbridge, then a trip on the 'auto-train' from the town station to the junction. I also spent some time at Blakedown station, which was a 6-mile bike ride from my home in Halesowen. I did take a few pictures in those days, but only perhaps one or two per visit – remember that photography was an expensive hobby for a lad still at school. Fortunately I kept the negatives and I am using a few of the pictures in this book; I hope that you will forgive the technical quality but enjoy the nostalgia. Also remember that most of these pictures were taken nearly 50 years ago.

Finally, the Severn Valley line from Hartlebury/Kidderminster to Bewdley is included here, but are covered in far greater depth in my *British Railways Past and Present Special: The Severn Valley Railway*, while Broadway is featured in my *Past and Present Special: Snow Hill to Cheltenham*.

Roger Siviter
Evesham

Past and present: ex-GWR 4-6-0, 'King' Class No 6024 *King Edward I*, crosses the River Avon as it leaves Evesham for Didcot on the evening of 1 May 1999. *RS*

Western Birmingham:
Old Hill, Halesowen and Dudley

LANGLEY GREEN: Our journey starts at Langley Green (Oldbury) in the north of the county. This area is now in the West Midlands but was originally in Worcestershire, on the western borders of the city of Birmingham. On 25 January 1984 the 1415 Kidderminster to Birmingham New Street service departs from Langley Green. Originally this GWR line ran into Birmingham Snow Hill, joining the Paddington-Wolverhampton line at Handsworth Junction, but with the closure of Snow Hill in 1972 trains ran into New Street via Galton Junction until the new Snow Hill station was opened in 1987.

To the left of the DMU can be seen the line that ran into the original Oldbury station, half a mile to the north, and just beyond that Oldbury goods station. The passenger station closed in 1915 but the goods station remained open until the mid-1980s. In pre-grouping days Langley Green station was known as Langley Green & Rood End, and the sidings that can be seen under the road bridge were known as Rood End sidings, serving the adjacent BIP chemical works. To the north of Oldbury, near West Bromwich on the LMS Birmingham-Wolverhampton line, was the other Oldbury station, nowadays known as Sandwell.

The 'present' view of Langley Green was taken on Saturday 13 March 1999, and shows Class 150 No 150102 departing as the 1312 Worcester Foregate Street to Dorridge via Birmingham Snow Hill service. The signal box and semaphore signals have now gone and the short branch to Oldbury goods, although still in place, is now out of use. Factory buildings still dominate the background of this Black Country scene. *Both RS*

9

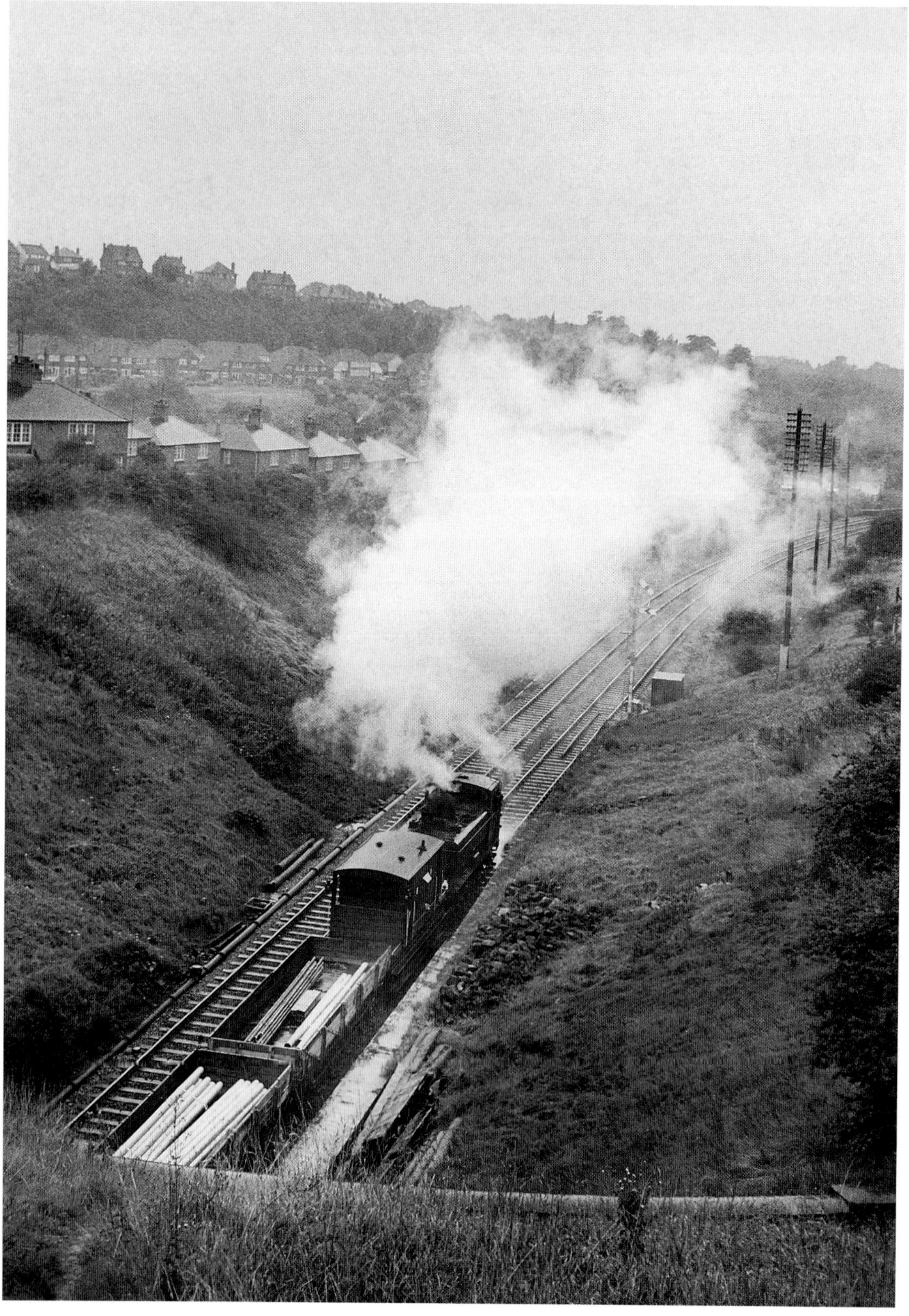

OLD HILL TUNNEL: Travelling south-westwards, after passing through Rowley Regis station the line descends steeply to Old Hill, passing through Old Hill Tunnel. In steam days freight trains usually required assistance for the climb from Old Hill to Rowley Regis, and on the evening of 11 August 1966 an unidentified ex-GWR 0-6-0 pannier tank banks a Halesowen-Langley goods (hauled by ex-GWR 0-6-0 pannier tank No 4646) up the steep grade just south of Old Hill Tunnel, the top of the entrance of which can be seen in the foreground.
 The 'present' picture, taken on 13 March 1990, shows DMU No 150108 climbing the steep bank out of Old Hill with the 1428 Stourbridge Junction to Dorridge service. Apart from a little more undergrowth, not a lot seems to have changed in nearly 33 years except that, of course, modern diesel-hauled goods trains nowadays rarely need banking assistance, and colour lights have replaced the semaphore signals. *Both RS*

11

OLD HILL (1): Just before Old Hill station the line crosses one of the Black Country's many canals, in this case the Dudley Canal, which runs from that town southwards to Halesowen. On the bridge on 21 April 1982 is a neat-looking Class 116 three-car diesel multiple unit (DMU) set forming a midday Stourbridge Junction to Birmingham New Street service.

Apart from the style of the DMU, very little in today's equivalent picture, taken on 13 March 1999, appears to have changed. No 150116 heads for Birmingham Snow Hill with the 1412 Worcester Foregate Street to Leamington Spa service. The train is due in Leamington at 1557, having taken 105 minutes for the 51-mile journey. *Both RS*

OLD HILL (2): Old Hill was the junction for the line to Blower's Green, Dudley, to the north and that to Halesowen to the south. From Halesowen the latter ran through to Longbridge, where it joined the Birmingham-Bristol main line; from Old Hill to Halesowen it was originally GWR, then joint GWR and Midland Railway to Longbridge. The line opened in 1883 but closed to passenger traffic between Old Hill and Halesowen in 1927, and from Halesowen to Longbridge even earlier, although the Austin factory workmen's trains from Old Hill to Longbridge ran until 1958. The Halesowen-Longbridge section closed in 1963 and the Old Hill-Halesowen line in 1969. The Halesowen branch was in Worcestershire but the line from Old Hill to Rowley Regis was in Staffordshire.

On 22 August 1966 ex-GWR pannier tank 0-6-0 No 3619 with an afternoon Halesowen to Stourbridge goods train leaves the branch's short Old Hill Tunnel and rounds the curve into Old Hill station. At the rear of the train is pannier tank No 4646, not only to provide banking assistance up the steep incline from Halesowen to the tunnel, but also to work the train forward to Stourbridge Junction yard (with No 3619 then at the rear).

The same location on 13 March 1999 is a timber yard with only the background trees as a point of reference with the 'past' picture. *Both RS*

13

HALESOWEN (1): On 10 May 1966 ex-GWR 0-6-0 pannier tank No 9608 is seen shunting at Halesowen. In the left background is Somers Steel Works, which had a rail-connected canal basin, while on the right can be seen the station and goods shed.

The site of Halesowen station and goods yard is now a factory estate with only the factory chimney as a comparison with the 'past' view. This picture was taken by courtesy of Brinton Bros (Boilers) Ltd on 13 March 1999. *Both RS*

HALESOWEN (2): Now in the station and looking back in the opposite direction, we see 0-6-0 pannier tank No 9774 pausing between shunting duties by the overgrown platforms on 2 June 1966. In the distance can be seen the steep climb up to Old Hill.

Although the whole area is now a factory estate, Somers Steel Works is still there to identify the location on 13 March 1999. *Both RS*

15

HALESOWEN (3): This view of the southern end of the station, looking towards Longbridge, was taken on 12 March 1966 and shows ex-GWR Class '5700' 0-6-0 pannier tank No 8718 taking a breather between shunting duties. The joint GWR/Midland line can be seen running under the road bridge carrying the Stourbridge-Halesowen-Birmingham road (A458), although by this time, the Longbridge-Halesowen section having closed in 1963, the line finished a few yards further on.

Today's picture shows that the site of this end of the station has been gradually filled in to join the A458, known locally as Mucklow Hill. On 13 March 1999 the top of the road bridge can just be seen in the centre of the picture, and to its right the corrugated factory roof. *Both RS*

RUBERY: The Halesowen to Longbridge section of the line passed through two stations, Hunnington (for many years home of the Bluebird Toffee factory) and Rubery, and between them was Dowery Dell viaduct. Shortly after leaving Halesowen station the very fine Manor Abbey athletics and cycling stadium was passed (it was close to the ruins of the 12th-century Halesowen Manor Abbey). The stadium opened in the late 1940s and attracted large crowds, especially for the cycling events where many top-class cyclists of the day, including the world sprint champion Reg Harris and many others from all over Europe, would participate. I attended many of these meetings, being a keen cyclist myself (my father had been Midland area sprint champion in the 1920s and '30s, as well as representing England at the Herne Hill meeting of champions). On several occasions the local goods train, hauled by a Midland '2F' 0-6-0, would pause by the ground for the crew to enjoy the proceedings (the line was just higher than the cycling and running track, giving a marvellous view). According to my 1948 Ian Allan number book, ex-LMS 0-6-0 Nos 58138 (LMS number 22947), 58143 (22955) and 58147 (22965) were seen regularly on the branch.

This vintage view of Rubery station (facing Longbridge) was taken on 10 July 1939. Although this section was joint GWR/LMS, earlier Midland Railway features predominate. At the station site on 13 March 1999 the trackbed is now a walkway. *R. S. Carpenter collection/RS*

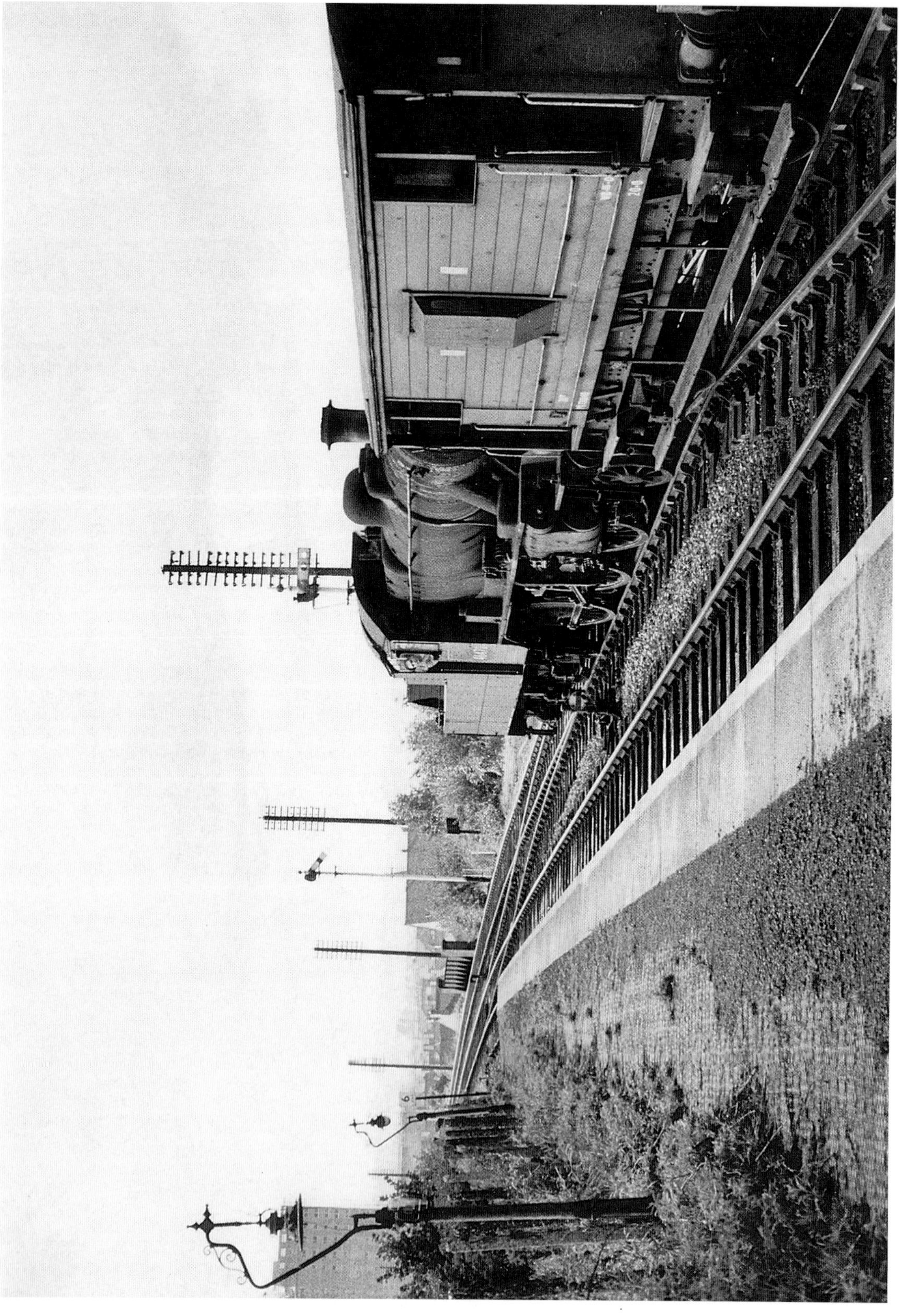

OLD HILL: Leaving the Halesowen branch and returning to the Birmingham to Stourbridge line, we see ex-LMS '2MT' 2-6-0 No 46470 banking a Stourbridge-Halesowen goods, hauled by 0-6-0 pannier tank No 4696, into Old Hill station on 2 September 1966. The junction to Halesowen was just east of the station, while the junction for Blowers Green and Dudley can be seen clearly under the brake-van. The second station at Old Hill – High Street – was situated on this branch about half a mile from the main station; the line closed to passenger traffic in 1964 and completely in 1968. Note the branch line signal and the ornate station lamps.

Today's view shows that all trace of the branch to Blowers Green has long gone, but the tower block on the left is still there, obscured by the trees, and new lamps have replaced the old ones. The train, formed of DMU No 150105, is the 1458 Stourbridge Junction to Birmingham Moor Street service, and the date is 13 March 1999. *Both RS*

19

CRADLEY HEATH is 9½ miles from Birmingham and 2½ miles from Stourbridge, and when this picture was taken on 15 February 1975 the station still had staggered platforms, that for Birmingham being behind the photographer; a level crossing divided the station, controlled by the signal box on the right. Waiting to depart from the Stourbridge platform is a pair of Western Region three-car DMUs forming the 1.14pm Lichfield City to Kidderminster service. Nowadays the cross-country route from Lichfield is via the electrified line through Birmingham New Street to Redditch.

Today's scene shows the new conventionally arranged Cradley Heath station (opened in 1984) with Class 150 No 150214 about to depart in the Stourbridge direction with the 1130 Stratford-upon-Avon to Great Malvern service on 14 March 1999. The ubiquitous factory buildings, so much a part of the Black Country landscape, are still very much in evidence, although probably not so prolific as 25/30 years ago. *Michael Mensing/RS*

LYDE GREEN (1): Half a mile after passing through Cradley Health station the line runs through Lyde Green (near Quarry Bank), where on 15 September 1966 a pair of Class '2MT' 2-6-0s, Nos 46457 and 46428, run past the signal box heading for Stourbridge shed. As they are back-to-back they have probably been working on the Halesowen branch. Unlike Cradley Heath, which was in Staffordshire, this area through to Stourbridge Junction is in Worcestershire again.

It was not possible to take the 'present' picture from quite the same angle as the 'past' scene. However, this picture, taken on 14 March 1999, shows the rear of DMU No 150101, forming the 1225 Worcester Shrub Hill to Leamington Spa service, passing the site of the old GWR signal box. *Both RS*

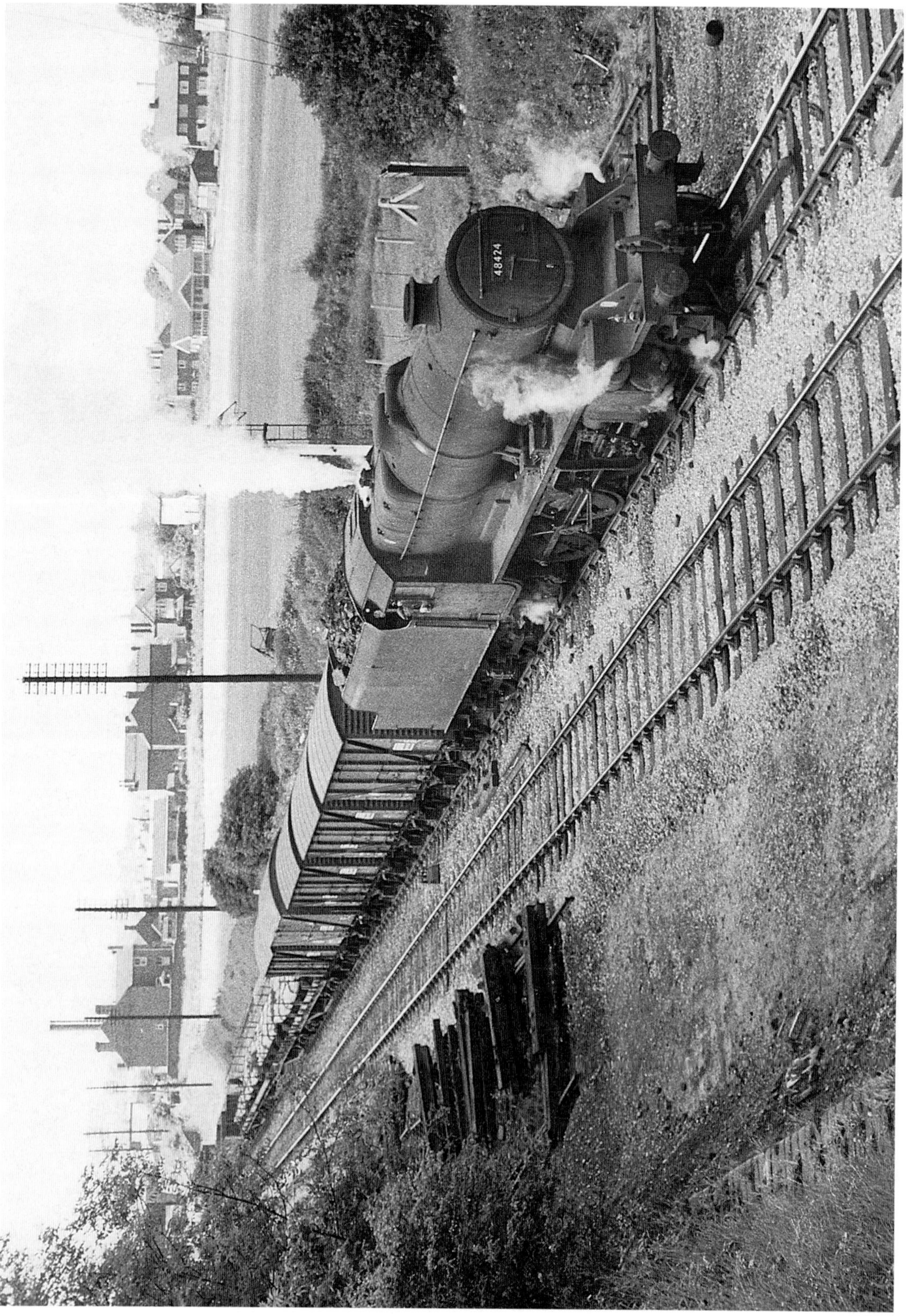
48424

LYDE GREEN (2): Turning round from the previous pictures, we see ex-LMS '8F' 2-8-0 No 48424 heading for the Birmingham area with a mixed goods train including some banana vans on 3 June 1966. In anticipation of the nearby Old Hill incline, the train is banked by '8F' No 48121. On the left is an old goods platform, its sidings in the process of being dismantled.

If you were lucky today you might see an '8F' 2-8-0 on a special charter, but otherwise, apart from a few freight workings, the line is monopolised by Class 150 DMUs. On 14 March 1999 No 150126 approaches with the 1105 Great Malvern to Stratford-upon-Avon service. The site of the goods sidings is still there, and the boundary wall, but the open fields from the 'past' scene are now a new housing estate. *Both RS*

STOURBRIDGE JUNCTION SHED: After Lyde Green the line passes through Lye station before it joins the old Oxford, Worcester & Wolverhampton ('Worse & Wear') line at Stourbridge Junction. Just north of the junction on the Wolverhampton line was Stourbridge Junction shed, in the area known locally as Amblecote. This former GWR shed was originally coded 84F, but when transferred to the London Midland Region of BR it became 2C. It closed by the end of 1966. The roundhouse, with its 28 radiating roads, was home mainly to freight locomotives and passenger tank engines, as well as a variety of pannier tanks for shunting and local trip workings, etc. On Sunday 13 March 1966 an assortment of goods locomotives can be seen, including '8F' 2-8-0s Nos 48412, 48121, 48468 and 48550, and Standard Class '5' 4-6-0 No 73069 on the right.

At the site of Stourbridge shed on 14 March 1999 we have Gooch Close and Churchward Close as pleasant reminders of the past. Other roads are named Dean Close, Armstrong Close and Collett Close, also names of GWR Chief Mechanical Engineers. *Both RS*

24

Another view of the shed, taken on Sunday 3 July 1966. From left to right are ex-GWR 0-6-0 pannier tanks Nos 4696, 9641, 3619, 9614, 4646 and 8718. *RS*

BRETTELL LANE: We are now on the Stourbridge-Dudley-Wolverhampton line at Brettell Lane, a mile or so north of Stourbridge shed, and formerly the junction for the line to Wolverhampton via Wombourne, which closed in the mid-1960s. On 6 April 1966 '8F' 2-8-0 No 48531 heads through the remains of Brettell Lane station with a southbound coal train. Beyond the road bridge can be seen the junction signal box. The Wombourne route was used extensively during the war years as a Black Country avoiding line, and at its northern end joined the GWR Wolverhampton to Shrewsbury route just north of Wolverhampton near Dunstall Park.

Because of tall fencing it was not possible to take the present-day equivalent picture from the same spot, so this more elevated view of Brettell Lane station site, taken on Sunday 14 March 1999, shows the line to Round Oak with the remains of the old signal box just visible under the road bridge. Colour lights have replaced the semaphore signals, but the factories are still there. *Both RS*

26

ROUND OAK STEEL WORKS, BRIERLEY HILL: On 4 March 1983 two Class 20 diesels, Nos 20070 and 20091, pass the edge of the steel works with a midday Bescot to Gloucester goods via Dudley, Stourbridge and Worcester Shrub Hill. This was always a lengthy train that produced a variety of motive power, including Class 25s, 37s and 40s, as well as the Class 20s seen here. Note the extensive sidings and the GWR signal box. Originally there were passenger stations at Round Oak and Brierley Hill, but these had closed by the early 1960s, the route closing to passengers by 1964.

Today Round Oak Steel Works is no longer with us, and most of the large site has become Merry Hill Shopping Centre, one of the largest in the country. This picture, taken on 7 March 1999, shows many changes, particularly regarding the trackwork. Most of the sidings have gone and, of course, the signal box and some semaphore signals. Where the bulk of the famous steel works was situated off the right-hand side of the picture is now the equally famous shopping centre. In March 1993 this through route to Dudley, Wolverhampton and Walsall, which opened in the 1850s, was truncated at Round Oak, although it will be seen in subsequent pictures that the track is only just being taken up, and in some places is still in situ. The reason for this is that Centro had plans to run a Midland Metro to the shopping centre, but these plans have still to come to fruition. This area thus remains the terminal of the line from Stourbridge Junction with very little traffic compared with when it was a through route. *Both RS*

27

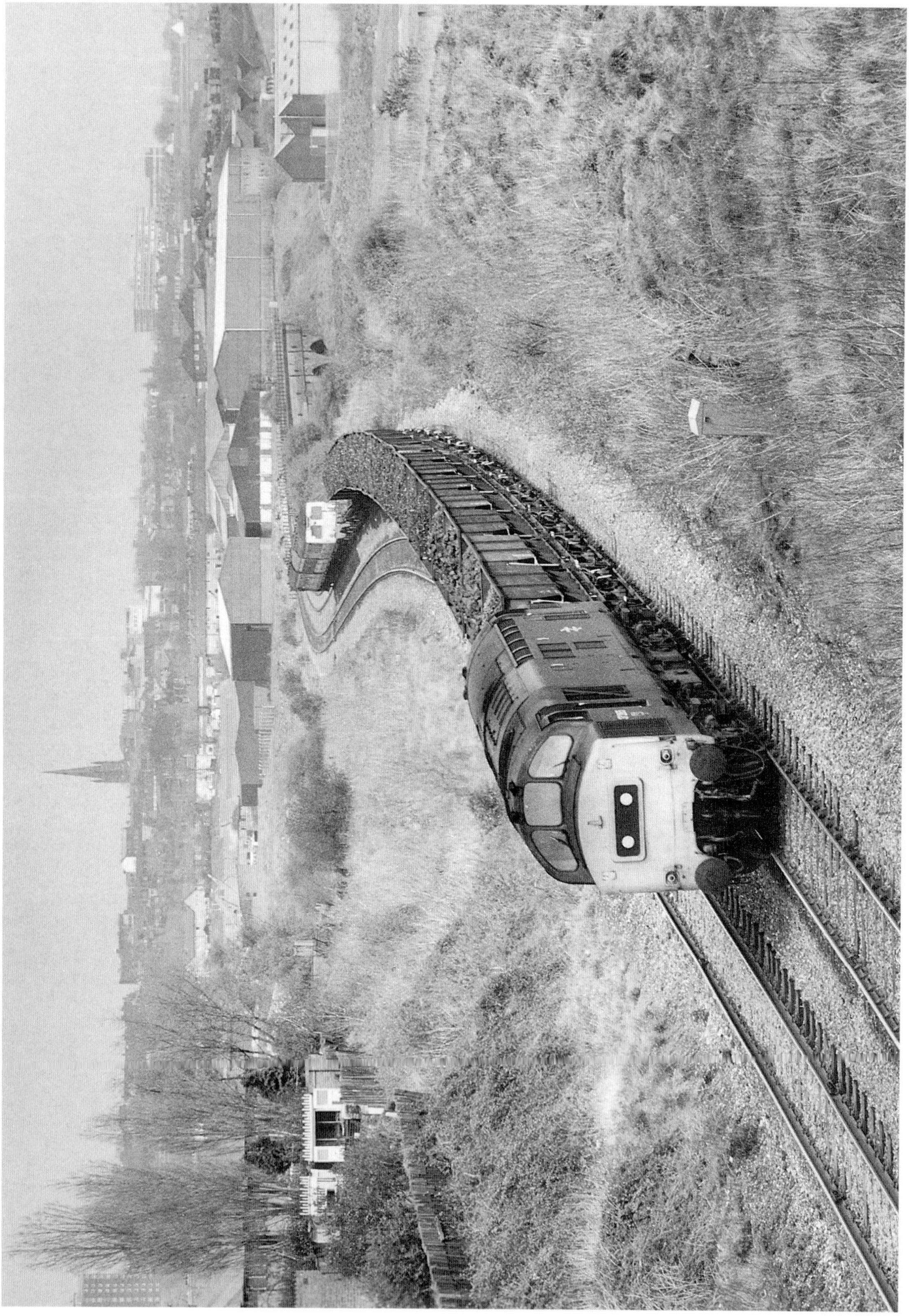

NEAR NETHERTON: On 4 May 1983, between Round Oak and Dudley, Class 37 No 37265 heads for Stourbridge Junction with the midday Bescot-Gloucester goods, which includes a DMU set. Dudley can be seen in the background with Dudley's 'Top Church' dominating the skyline. From north of Stourbridge Junction the line has been in Staffordshire, but within a few hundred yards it will be running through Dudley and thus back into Worcestershire.

The 'present' scene in March 1999 shows the trackwork in the process of being dismantled, and the attractive pigeon lofts on the left of the 'past' picture have now gone. In the Black Country, as in most working class areas, keeping racing pigeons is a very popular hobby. *Both RS*

29

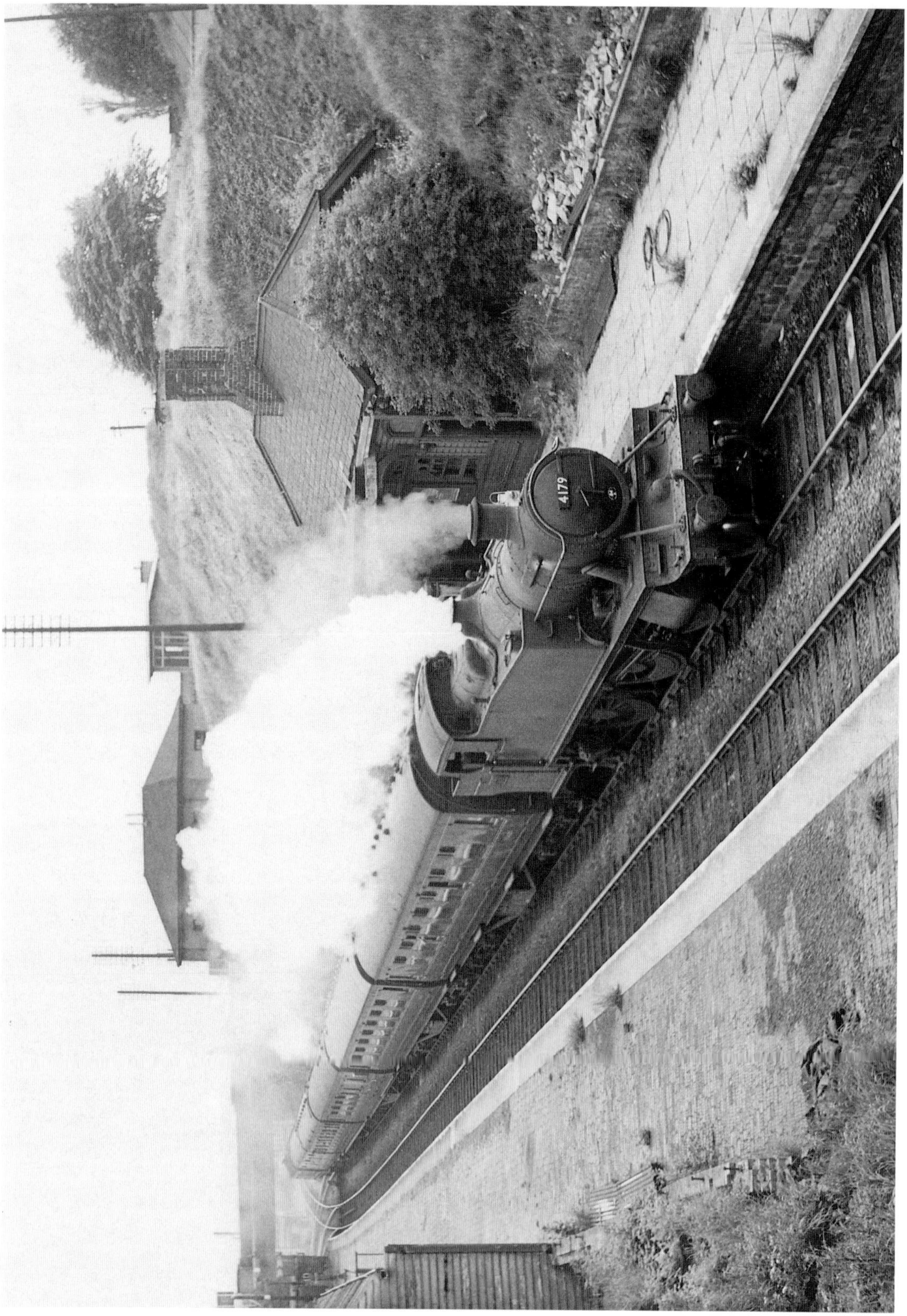
4179

BLOWERS GREEN, on the outskirts of Dudley, is our next location, where the branch line from Old Hill met the Stourbridge-Dudley line. On Whit Monday, 11 June 1962, ex-GWR Class '5100' 2-6-2T No 4179 arrives at the station with a return Worcester-Stourbridge-Wolverhampton Low Level excursion. At the rear of the train, coming in from the left, can be seen the line from Old Hill.

When Blowers Green was revisited on 7 March 1999 the track was still in place and the old booking office was still there. Because of excavation work it was not possible to copy the 'past' picture from the same angle to show where the branch from Old Hill came in; this branch opened in 1878, and closed completely in 1968. *Michael Mensing/Christina Siviter*

DUDLEY: This panoramic view of Dudley station looking towards Wolverhampton was taken in the late 1950s and shows ex-GWR Class '5700' 0-6-0 pannier tank No 8742 in the bay platform. In its heyday Dudley was a very busy station, with local traffic to Wolverhampton and Walsall, as well as to Birmingham (both via Swan Village and Old Hill) and Stourbridge. In summer months it also saw a good deal of excursion traffic from all over the country to Dudley's famous zoo and castle. I well remember being told of someone from Dudley who was on holiday in Blackpool and took a railway mystery excursion only to finish up at Dudley Zoo! The station was next door to these attractions as well as Dudley Hippodrome, where, in its prime, stars from all over the world would entertain large audiences. All passenger traffic to Dudley ceased by 1964, the Wolverhampton section having been closed to passengers in 1962. The station site was turned into a freightliner terminal, but this was closed in 1986.

This is the derelict scene at Dudley today with some trackwork and, on the right, some brickwork to identify with the 'past' view. The existing trackwork is part of the line to Dudley Port and Walsall, the trackbed of the Wolverhampton line being on the left. *R. S. Carpenter collection/ RS*

Stourbridge

STOURBRIDGE JUNCTION (1): We now return to Stourbridge Junction, where the line from Birmingham Snow Hill meets the line from Dudley, then heads southwards to Kidderminster and Worcester. On a wet October day in 1950, ex-GWR Class '4MT' 2-6-2 tank No 4104 heads south through the station. Behind the locomotive can be glimpsed the large goods yard, much of which was closed in 1966, together with the locomotive shed. Behind the sheds on the left runs the branch to Stourbridge Town and on to Stourbridge Basin; this last section closed in 1965 and all goods traffic ceased on the branch in the same year.

Today's view, taken on 9 February 1999, catches Class 150 DMU No 150001, the empty stock of the 1128 to Dorridge, entering the station from the sidings on the western side of the line, and shows many differences from the 'past' picture, taken almost 50 years earlier. The trackwork has been extensively altered; there is now no goods yard on the eastern side and only a few sidings opposite. The old semaphore signals have been replaced by colour lights, but the impressive signal box is still there, looking in good condition. Some of the sheds have gone, thus revealing clearly the branch to the Town station. The northbound platform has also been shortened. *Both RS*

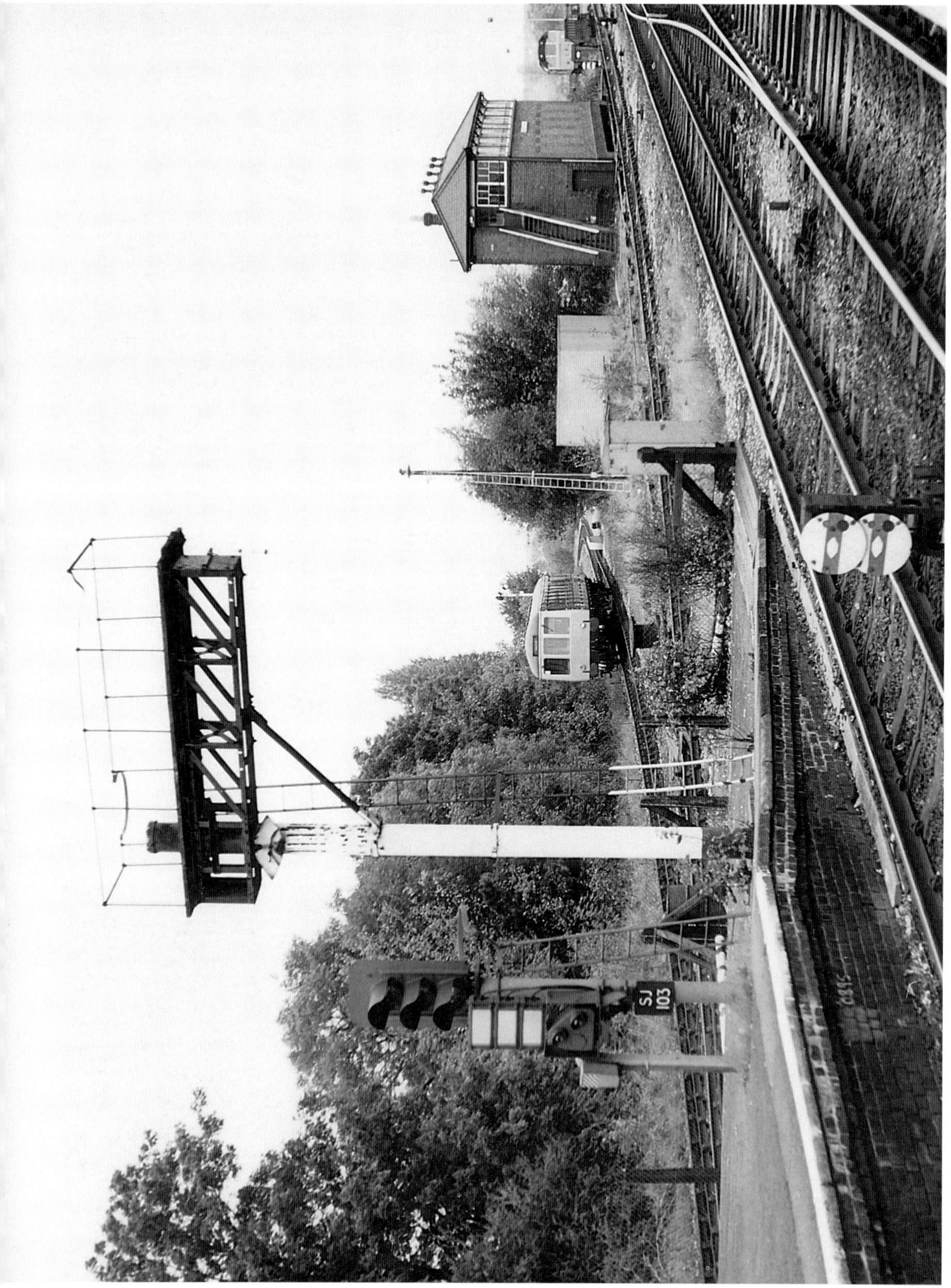
SJ 103

STOURBRIDGE JUNCTION (2): Although the Stourbridge to Dudley line opened in 1852 (part of the Oxford, Worcester & Wolverhampton Railway), the line from Stourbridge to Birmingham was not completed until 1867, and the short branch (less than a mile) to Stourbridge Town in 1879. On the afternoon of 28 October 1981, a single railcar enters the Junction station with the shuttle service from Town. Note the Class 25 diesel by the signal box, the remains of the bracket signal, and the new colour light signal.

On 9 February 1999 railcar No 153320 is seen in the same location with the 1127 service from the Town station. The most noticeable change over the 18 years is the modification of the colour light signal. This view also shows more clearly the few sidings that are now left. *Both RS*

35

STOURBRIDGE TOWN: For many years ex-GWR '1400' Class 0-4-2 tanks worked the Stourbridge Town branch, but by the beginning of the 1960s their duties were taken over by double-ended diesel railcars. On 11 June 1962 (Whit Monday) railcar No 55006 leaves Stourbridge Town station with the 3.40pm to Stourbridge Junction. The Town station had just one platform, the line on the right being that for Stourbridge Basin.

Today the line has been singled and the platform is on the right-hand. Also, because the line now terminates at the station, the footbridge has been done away with. On 9 February 1999 single unit No 153320 departs from the Town station with the 1347 service to the Junction. *Michael Mensing/RS*

STOURBRIDGE JUNCTION (3): Ex-GWR 'Hall' Class 4-6-0 No 5943 *Elmdon Hall* and an unidentified '5100' Class 2-6-2 tank stand in the carriage sidings at the eastern side of Stourbridge Junction station in August 1952. On 9 February 1999 the carriage sidings are a distant memory, and in their place is a vast car park for rail commuters. *Both RS*

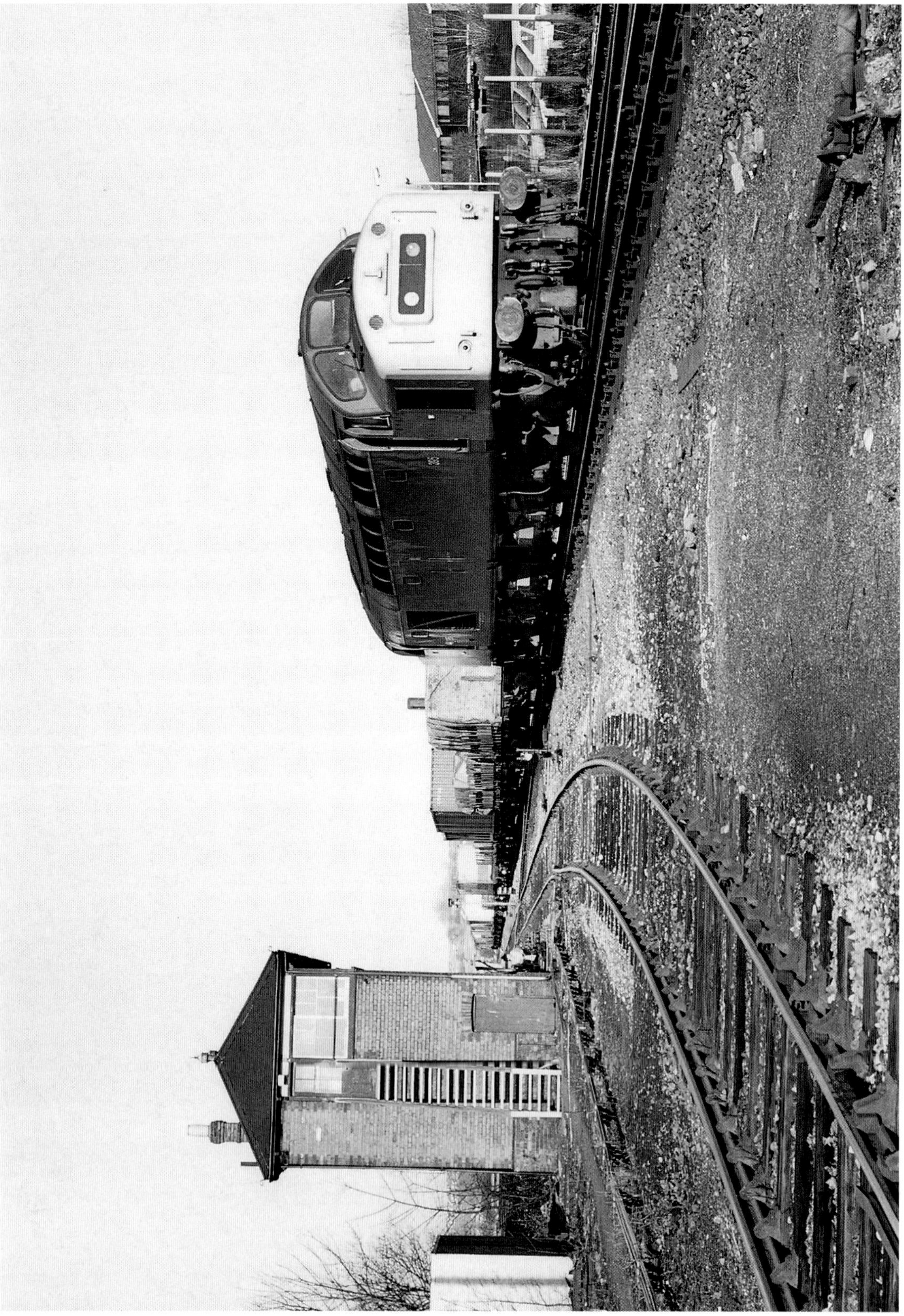

STOURBRIDGE JUNCTION (4): On 18 January 1984 English Electric Class 40 diesel No 40195 heads south through Stourbridge Junction with a freightliner train from the Birmingham area.

Fifteen years later, on 9 February 1999, Class 150 DMU No 150019 enters the station with the empty stock for the 1158 to Birmingham Moor Street. Although there is a regular service to Worcester and Hereford, many trains from the Birmingham area terminate at Stourbridge, and within a few minutes (for change of platform, etc) they are leaving on their return workings. *Both RS*

STOURBRIDGE JUNCTION (5): The next picture was taken in October 1950 at the southern end of the station with, on the right, ex-GWR 'Hall' Class 4-6-0 No 6930 *Aldersey Hall* on an express for Worcester and Hereford, and, just visible on the left, a pannier tank on a push-and-pull train probably for the Town station. The Junction station consisted of two island platforms, both with large canopies and, as was quite common with larger stations, a refreshment room, as I well remember from my spotting days!

Today's view, taken on 9 February 1999, shows that the canopies have not only been replaced but also considerably shortened. The elegant 'Hall' Class locomotive has been replaced by a Class 150 unit – No 150101 – seen leaving with the 1022 Leamington Spa to Worcester Foregate Street service. *Both RS*

STOURBRIDGE JUNCTION (6): Our last scene at Stourbridge Junction shows how the style of diesel locomotive has changed over the last 15 years. The 'past' scene, taken on 18 January 1984, shows 'Peak' Class diesel No 45066 (introduced in 1959) at the head of a mainly coil train bound for Wolverhampton. At the rear of the train is Brush Type 2 diesel No 31126, which was the leading engine from Birmingham, the train having reversed at the Junction.

On 9 February 1999 brand new Class 66 diesel No 66051 (which had only arrived from Canada a few weeks earlier, on 5 January) heads through the station with a northbound goods. The scene itself has not changed a great deal, but the 'Peaks' finished service around the mid-1980s and the Class 31s are now a diminishing band. *Both RS*

Through Kidderminster to Worcester

HAGLEY (1): After leaving the industrial town of Stourbridge the line to Worcester runs south through the pleasant Worcestershire countryside to Hagley, some 2 miles from Stourbridge Junction. Early in the evening of 12 May 1966 ex-LMS Class '8F' 2-8-0 No 48424 (from Stourbridge shed, 2C) runs tender-first through the delightful ex-GWR Hagley station heading for Kidderminster in order to work the 8.10pm Kidderminster to Oxley goods. Note the fine-looking GWR footbridge, clearly visible beyond the road bridge, and the remains of the small goods yard on the right.

On 9 February 1999 trees obscure the railway, but in the centre of the picture, just above the trees, can be seen the road bridge and the station sign.

To complete this trio of views, we see '8F' 2-8-0 No 48424 again later the same day, working hard through Hagley station at about 8.30pm with the 8.10pm Kidderminster-Oxley goods. The photograph was taken from the signal box steps, at the invitation of the friendly signalman, who also supplied me with the information about the freight working. The box has long since gone, together with the semaphore signals. *All RS*

HAGLEY (2): On 3 March 1983 Class 37 No 37253 heads south through the station with the 1245 Walsall (Bescot) to Gloucester goods.

The 'present' view of Hagley, taken on 9 February 1999, shows that apart from the disappearance of the station building on the left, very little has changed. The platform canopy and remaining station building are still in very good order, and the GWR footbridge, which dates from 1884, must be one of the finest examples left in the country. The train, formed of Class 150 No 150216, is the 1325 Leamington Spa to Worcester Foregate Street service. *Both RS*

BLAKEDOWN (1): Just under 2 miles south of Hagley is Blakedown station, formerly known as Churchill & Blakedown. This is where as a young lad I spent many happy hours, especially in the long summer holidays. On occasions I took a few pictures, including this one of ex-GWR 'Hall' Class 4-6-0 No 6950 *Kingthorpe Hall* as it called at Churchill & Blakedown in August 1950 with a semi-fast from Birmingham Snow Hill to Worcester, Hereford and possibly Cardiff; from the angle of the sun it is mid-afternoon. 'Hall' Class locomotives were the mainstay of this route. *Kingthorpe Hall*, built in 1942 and scrapped in 1964, was shedded at Worcester (85A) at the time, but its latter years were spent at 88A, Cardiff East Dock. Note the edge of the crossing gates on the extreme right, and the ex-GWR coaching stock.

There is no 'Hall' in today's picture, taken on 9 February 1999, as No 150210 runs through Blakedown station with the 1443 Birmingham New Street-Hereford service. A modern 'bus shelter' has replaced the old station and there are also modern crossing barriers – however, the old signal box (behind the photographer) is still there. *Both RS*

45

BLAKEDOWN (2): Turning round from the previous pictures, we see ex-GWR 'Modified Hall' Class 4-6-0 No 6984 *Owsden Hall* with a morning Paddington-Worcester-Stourbridge Junction train in August 1950. This train arrived at Stourbridge at around 1.00pm, returning at 4.00pm. Occasionally, if I was lucky, the train engine would be one of Hawksworth's 'County' Class 4-6-0s. Note the GWR stock and interesting-looking van immediately behind the tender, as well as the track leading to the small goods yard on the left.

At roughly the same spot, only this time including the signal box, we see a pair of English Electric Class 20s, Nos 20096 and 20025, on a special from Bristol to Birmingham New Street, one of a series of charter trains organised by Pathfinder Tours in connection with Gloucester BR open day on 1 July 1990. The goods yard has long since gone. *Both RS*

KIDDERMINSTER: The next location is the carpet town of Kidderminster, some 18¾ miles from Birmingham. This area is dealt with extensively in my *British Railways Past and Present Special: The Severn Valley Railway*, but I have included this picture of the lovely old Tudor-style station at Kidderminster, taken around 1958-59, as a pleasant reminder of the past.

Sadly, this charming old timber station was burned down some years ago, and replaced with a modern functional building, as seen on 2 September 1994. *R. S. Carpenter collection/RS*

47

BEWDLEY: Part of the Severn Valley line from Kidderminster to Victoria Bridge, the boundary with Shropshire, north of Bewdley, is in Worcestershire, but, as explained in the Introduction, it is extensively covered in my *British Railways Past and Present Special: The Severn Valley Railway*, as is the line to Tenbury and Bewdley-Stourport-Hartlebury, etc. However, I have included this picture of ex-LMS '8F' 2-8-0 No 48531 as it trundled through Bewdley station on 30 June 1966 with a heavy coal train from Highley (Alveley Colliery) to Stourport power station.

48

The 'present' equivalent was taken on 14 March 1999. In the distance is Class '2MT' 2-6-0 No 46521 propelling a brake-van in the Kidderminster direction. Now in preservation, much has been added to the location over the last 33 years, but the basic scene remains the same. *Both RS*

THE SEVERN VALLEY RAILWAY: What better way to portray the line in its preserved state than to show two pictures of illustrious visitors? Former GWR 'City' Class 4-4-0 No 3440 *City of Truro* heads for Bewdley with an afternoon train from Bridgnorth on 21 June 1986. The location is Northwood, just south of Victoria Bridge, and near the trackbed of the junction for Tenbury Wells and Woofferton. *RS*

The second scene shows 'Castle' Class 4-6-0 No 7029 *Clun Castle* crossing the Severn at Victoria Bridge on 20 June 1982 with a Bewdley-Bridgnorth train. The river marks the boundary between Worcestershire and Shropshire. *RS*

HARTLEBURY: Back again on the former GWR Snow Hill-Kidderminster-Worcester line, we arrive at Hartlebury, formerly the junction for Stourport and Bewdley on the Severn Valley line to Shrewsbury. At 1425 on 19 October 1983 a rare visitor to the line, Class 46 diesel No 46017, climbs the steep grade to Hartlebury from Kidderminster (some 4 miles to the north) with a heavy southbound coal train. On the right is the Baggeridge brickworks, complete with splendid chimney.

On 2 January 1999 ex-LMS Class '8F' 2-8-0 No 48773 pounds up to Hartlebury with a return special charter from Tyseley to Kidderminster, Worcester and Gloucester, the outward working having been via Bromsgrove and up the famous Lickey Bank. Only the factory complex appears to have changed over the intervening years, but the chimney is still there – slightly modified – and there is new fencing as the factory has taken over some railway land. *Both RS*

52

DROITWICH: Some 5½ miles south of Hartlebury is the famous spa town of Droitwich, where the line from Stourbridge and Kidderminster joins the line linking Droitwich with the Birmingham-Bristol main line just south of Bromsgrove. On a wintery 16 January 1985, DMU No 51131 enters Droitwich station with a Birmingham New Street-Kidderminster-Worcester Foregate Street-Great Malvern service. The line to Bromsgrove diverges to the right of the signal box. Note also the coal sidings where, at that time, a small industrial diesel locomotive was employed.

The 'present' view, taken on 23 May 1998, shows that the coal sidings/yard have now gone but that the fine GWR signals still remain. Unit No 150127 forms the 1510 New Street to Great Malvern via Bromsgrove service. *Both RS*

RAINBOW HILL TUNNEL: The only station between Droitwich and Worcester was Fernhill Heath, which, like Cutnall Green between Hartlebury and Droitwich, was never busy and closed many years ago (see *British Railways Past and Present Special: The Severn Valley Railway*). Before the line arrives at Worcester Tunnel Junction, where the Shrub Hill and Foregate Street lines divide, it runs through Rainbow Hill Tunnel, where these three views were taken. In the first ex-LMS Class '5' 4-6-0 No 45040 heads out of the tunnel with a northbound evening parcels train on 15 May 1965.

The 'present' view shows DMU No 158794 emerging from the tunnel with the 1649 Worcester Shrub Hill to Birmingham New Street service on 28 August 1994.

To complete this trio of pictures, English Electric Class 37 diesels Nos 37177 and 37508 are seen in close-up as they burst out of the short tunnel and head for Bromsgrove for banking duties on the Lickey Bank on the evening of 12 September 1986. Although today there is no banking up the Lickey, in the 1980s assistance was often required for heavy night-time and sleeper trains, and Class 37s, which were 'shedded' at the remains of Worcester shed, were often called on for these duties. Living in Bromsgrove at the time and fairly near to the line, I was often woken up between midnight and 1.00am by the sound of a train being banked up the Lickey by a pair of Class 37s. *Michael Mensing/RO (2)*

54

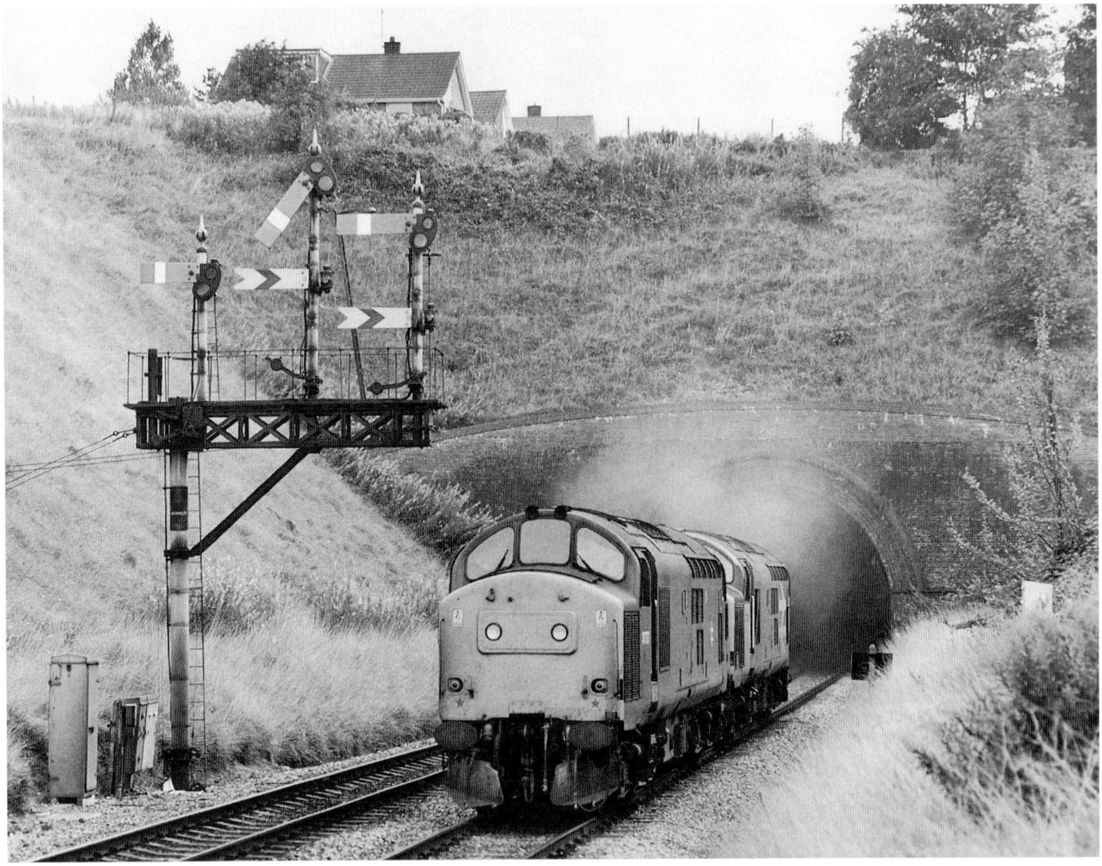

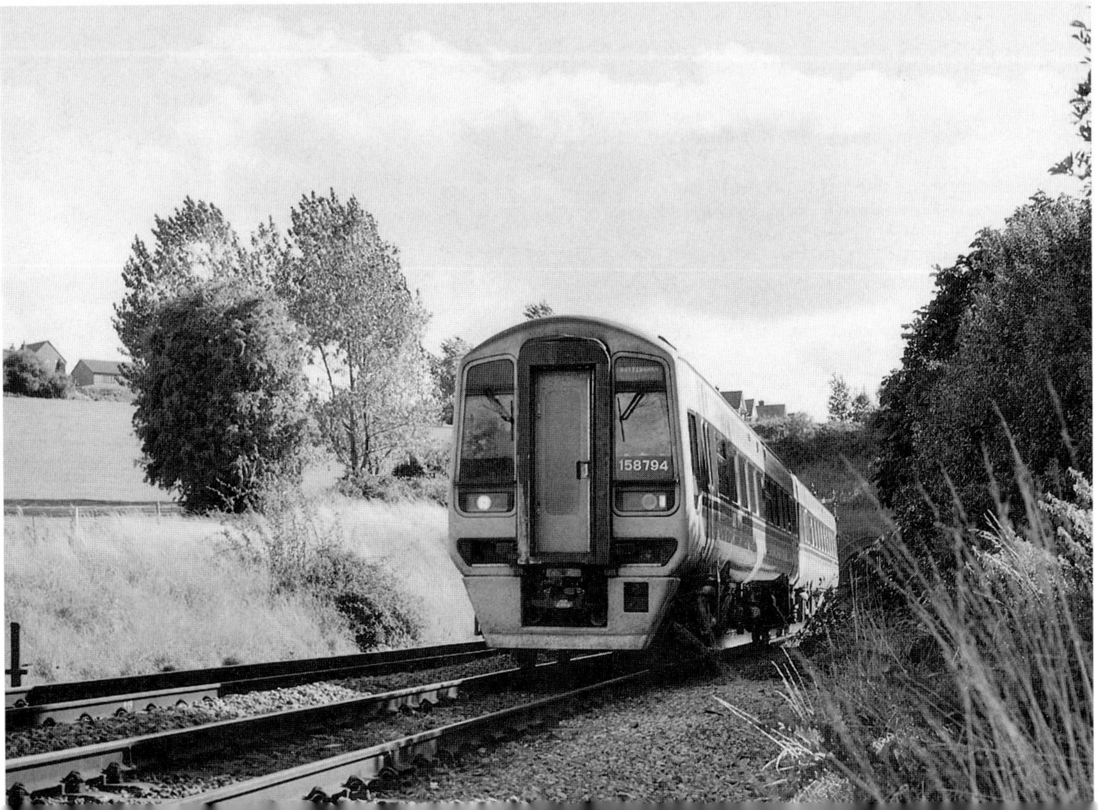
158794

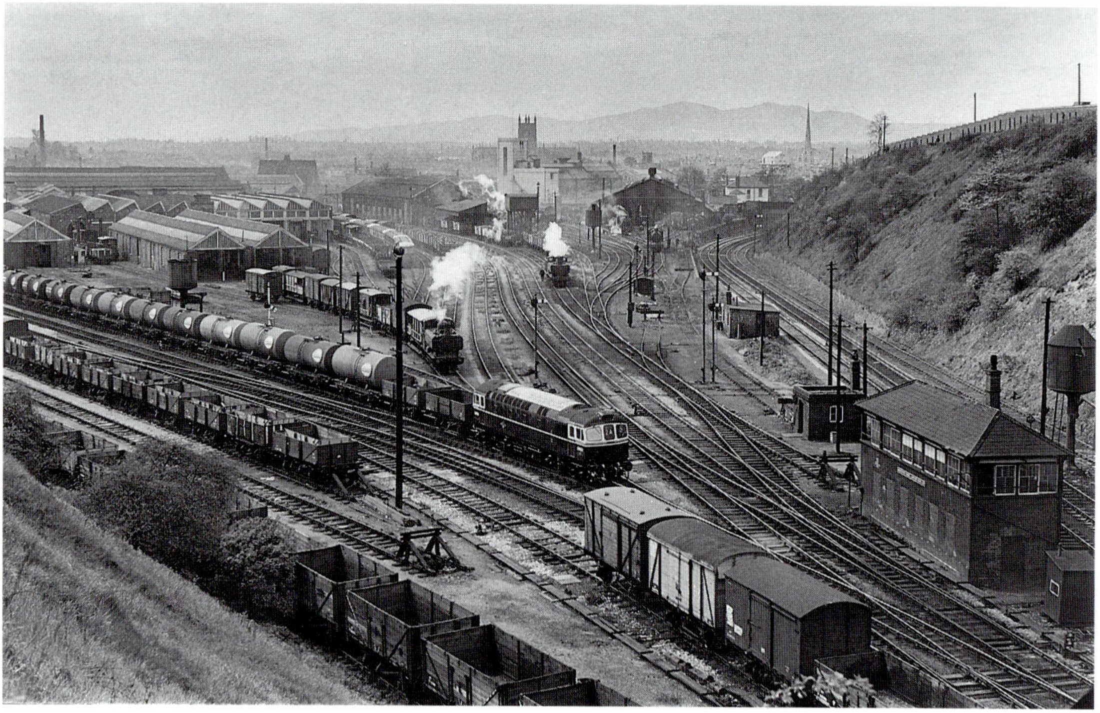

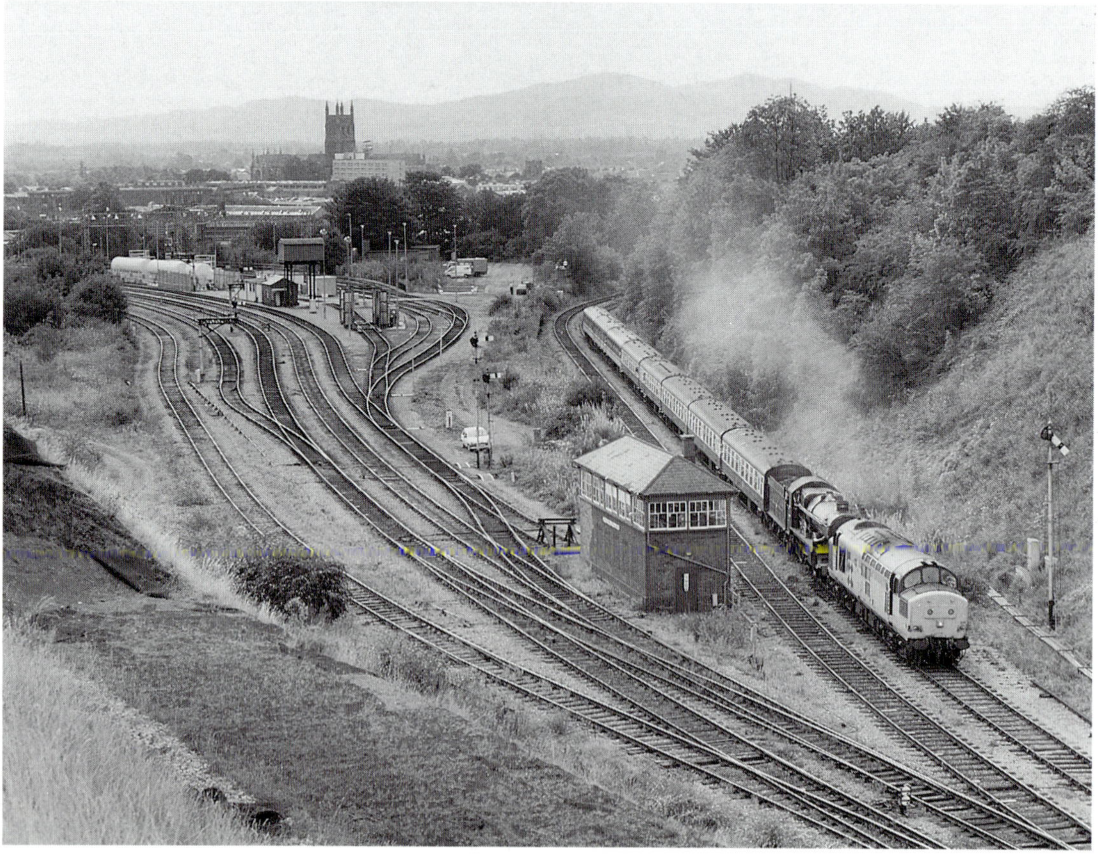

WORCESTER TUNNEL JUNCTION: The first view of the Tunnel Junction area was taken on 30 April 1963 and shows Type 3 diesel locomotive (now Class 33) No 6521 heading north from the Shrub Hill direction with an Esso tank train, possibly from the Fawley refinery near Southampton. The lines in the centre lead to Shrub Hill station itself, and the locomotive repair works is on the left-hand side of these. The two locomotive sheds are on the right-hand side, and to the right of them is the line to Worcester Foregate Street, Malvern and Hereford. In addition, a short half-mile branch ran from the locomotive yard to the local vinegar works. One ex-GWR pannier tank shunts the goods shed, and another the locomotive coaling stage. In the centre of the picture, set against the Malvern Hills, is the tower of Worcester Cathedral, and in the bottom right-hand corner is the signal box that controls this junction area.

Today much has disappeared from the earlier scene – locomotive sheds and works, goods shed and a great deal of trackwork – but the signal box is still there and some semaphore signals. Part of the old shed area is a diesel refuelling point, and the tower by the old coaling stage is still in place. The train heading north from the Hereford direction is a Westbury-Bristol-Kidderminster special charter, headed by Class 37 No 37229 and ex-GWR 'Castle' Class 4-6-0 No 5029 *Nunney Castle* on 31 August 1996; the Class 37 is heading the train as a precaution against fire risk.

Finally, a telephoto lens shot at the same location catches BR Standard Class '8' 'Pacific' No 71000 *Duke of Gloucester* as it heads north on 30 October 1993 with a Didcot-Worcester-Kidderminster special. This shot highlights the signal box and the tight curves to the two Worcester stations. Behind the rear of the train is the direct line from Shrub Hill to Foregate Street, thus forming a triangle. *B. J. Ashworth/RS (2)*

Worcester Foregate Street to Malvern and Upton

FOREGATE STREET (1): We are now just to the east of Worcester Foregate Street station, where the Hereford line crosses the Birmingham-Worcester canal. On 7 May 1989 English Electric Class 50 No 50034 *Furious* climbs towards Worcester Shrub Hill station with the 1615 Hereford-Paddington service. This was the final year of Class 50 workings on the Paddington-Worcester-Hereford trains, their place being taken by Class 47s, then Turbo units.

By contrast, on 27 February 1999 a Centro Class 150 DMU heads for Foregate Street with the 1103 from Birmingham New Street, terminating at Foregate Street. *Both RS*

FOREGATE STREET (2): Worcester Foregate Street station, together with the line to Hereford, was opened in the 1850s, and via Kidderminster it is 33¼ miles from Birmingham, and 26¾ miles via Bromsgrove. 'Hall' Class 4-6-0 No 5952 *Cogan Hall* arrives at Foregate Street on 19 August 1962 with the 5.35pm Hereford to Paddington train.

Today much of the station remains unchanged. The GWR canopies are still in place, and semaphore signals still control the area. However, the footbridge has long gone, and these days to change platforms passengers have to negotiate dozens of steps down to the booking office, then more steps to get back up to the other side. Unit No 156419 leaves Foregate Street on 27 February 1999 with the 1153 Hereford to Birmingham New Street and Nottingham, via Stourbridge Junction, service. The high warehouse or factory building is still in place, but the station railings have gone, to be replaced by a wall. *Michael Mensing/RS*

59

SEVERN BRIDGE, WORCESTER: After leaving Foregate Street, the Hereford line crosses the River Severn near Worcester Racecourse before heading south-west for Malvern and Hereford, and these four views show various preserved locomotives on the bridge. In the first photograph it is ex-GWR 'Hall' Class 4-6-0 No 6998 *Burton Agnes Hall* with a Great Western Society special from Didcot to Hereford and return on 24 June 1973.

The second picture has three for the price of one as ex-GWR 'Hall' Class 4-6-0 No 4930 *Hagley Hall*, BR Standard Class '4' 2-6-4 tank No 80079 and ex-LMS Class '4MT' 2-6-0 No 43106 head for Hereford from the Severn Valley Railway for duty on the Welsh Marches route on Friday 18 February 1983. All three worked special trains on the two subsequent weekends (19 and 26 February), with Nos 80079 and 43106 working together.

In the third shot Class 50 No 50015 *Valiant* works the 1240 Hereford to Worcester train for the Open Day on 5 May 1991.

The final picture shows an illustrious visitor, ex-GWR 'King' Class 4-6-0 No 6024 *King Edward I*, as it crosses the Severn at Worcester on 27 September 1997 with a Gloucester-Worcester-Hereford-Newport special. The 'King' Class never worked this route in steam days, so this is probably the first occasion that a member of this famous class was seen at this location. *All RS*

61

SUCKLEY: Roughly halfway along the 7 miles between Worcester and Malvern Link was the junction for the Bromyard branch (which originally ran through to Leominster). This branch, which followed the valley of the River Teme, was a victim of the Beeching axe, closing in September 1964, the section from Bromyard to Leominster having closed in the 1950s. Suckley station was situated just inside the Worcestershire border, around 8 miles west of the City of Worcester. On 9 January 1962 a three-car Swindon DMU set pauses at the station with the 4.50pm Bromyard to Worcester service.

On 27 February 1999 only a much-extended station house remains to remind us of the former scene. *Michael Mensing/Christina Siviter*

MALVERN LINK: On 19 June 1960 ex-GWR Prairie tank No 4124 arrives at Malvern Link station with the 5.00pm Leamington Spa to Great Malvern train, passing the busy-looking goods yard and impressive GWR signal box. This station brings back mixed memories to me, for when I was doing my army service with the Band of the Worcestershire Regiment I would often return to Worcester by catching a mail/parcels train from Birmingham New Street at around 2.30-3.00am. One early morning in the summer of 1956, instead of getting out at Worcester Foregate Street I must have fallen asleep and, much to my dismay, woke up at Malvern Link and had to walk the 7 miles back to Worcester, before I could get a taxi back to Norton Barracks, where I arrived just in time for reveille!

Today's scene shows that the goods yards have now all closed, the signal box has gone and the platforms have been shortened. On 6 March 1999 Class 150 unit No 150002 approaches the station with the 1143 Birmingham New Street to Hereford service. *Michael Mensing/RS*

GREAT MALVERN station was much more confined than Malvern Link, with only a small bay platform at the southern end for the line to Ashchurch; the latter line closed as far as Upton-on-Severn in the 1950s, leaving a branch line from Ashchurch to Upton. In this delightful scene at Great Malvern on the morning of 9 May 1963 ex-GWR 'Castle' Class 4-6-0 No 7002 *Devizes Castle* enters the station with the up 'Cathedrals Express'. No 7002 was built in 1946, fitted with a double chimney in 1961 and withdrawn from service in 1964, its final shed being Worcester (85A).

Today most of the trains through Great Malvern are DMUs, as on 6 March 1999, with No 150017 entering the station forming the 1255 Hereford to Birmingham New Street service. However, apart from the signal box, semaphore signals and short siding into the old bay platform, the station still looks very much as it did. It still boasts a fine refreshment room (now privately run), which amongst other things sells railway books and pictures. Note also the way that people's clothing has changed over the years. *B. J. Ashworth/RS*

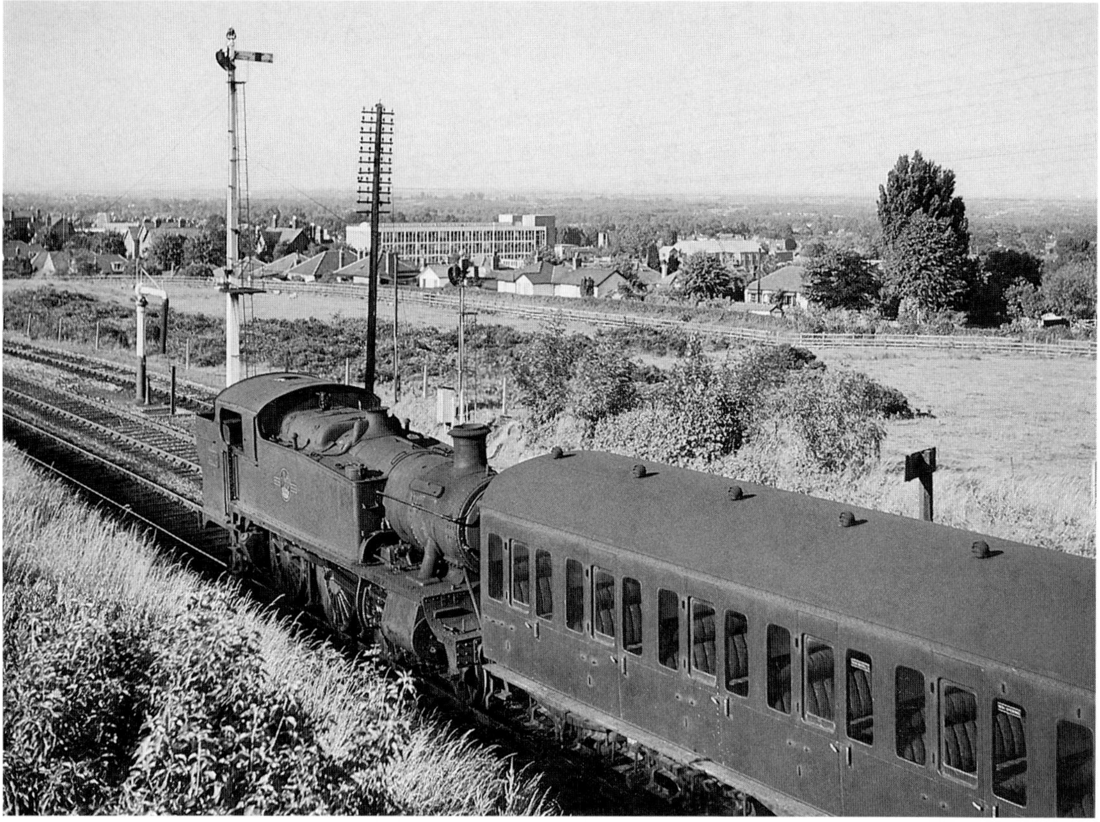

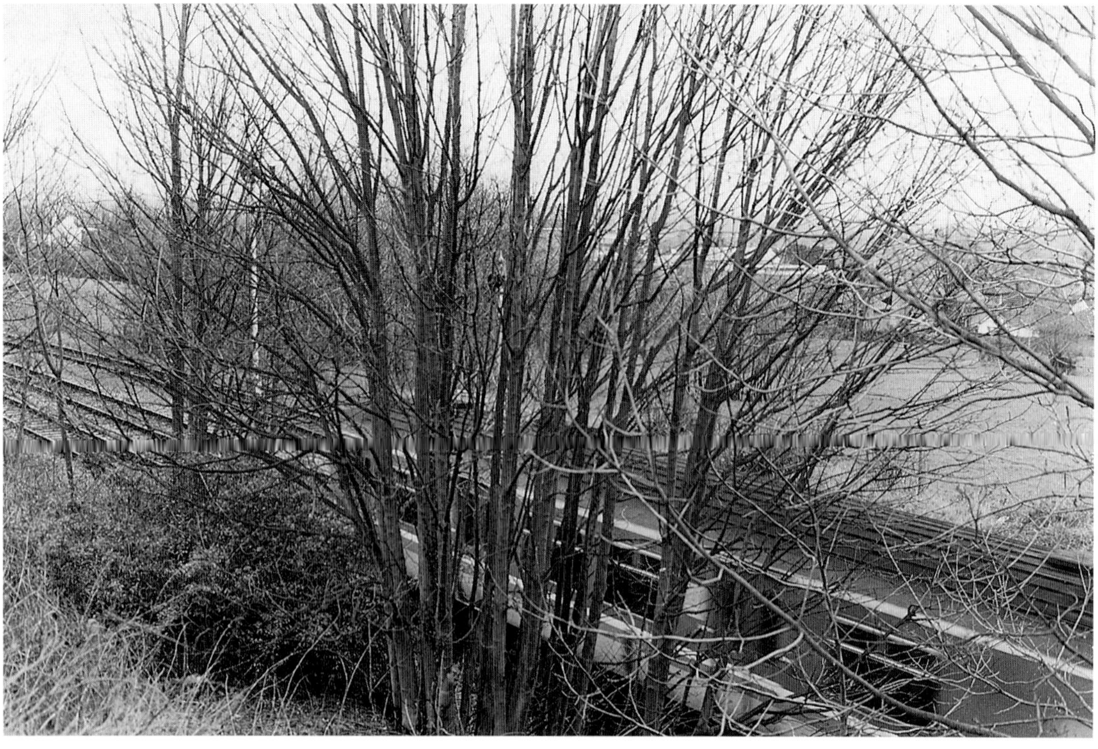

MALVERN WELLS: Our final views at Malvern are just north of Malvern Wells station. In the first 2-6-2T No 4172 leaves for Great Malvern with the empty stock for the 6.45pm to Birmingham, having earlier worked in with the 4.25pm from Snow Hill.

The equivalent view, taken through the tree growth on 6 March 1999, shows DMU No 150002 heading for Great Malvern with the 1353 Hereford-Birmingham New Street service. The loop line is still in place, as are the semaphore signals.

The third photograph, taken on 18 February 1983 from a slightly different angle, shows preserved locomotives Nos 4930, 80079 and 43106 en route to Hereford to work special charters on the Welsh Marches route (see page 60). At the rear of the three locomotives, on the right, is the trackbed of the branch to Upton-on-Severn and Ashchurch.

Just south of this location is Colwall Tunnel, which forms the boundary between Worcestershire and Herefordshire. *Michael Mensing/RS (2)*

UPTON-ON-SEVERN: The Malvern to Upton-on-Severn line closed in 1952, but Upton to Ashchurch survived until 1961, and Ashchurch to Tewkesbury until 1964. On 9 July 1955 ex-LMS Class '3F' 0-6-0 No 43645 and 3rd Class brake carriage No M25048M wait to leave the terminus at Upton as the 5.45pm service to Ashchurch. Note the decorations in the brickwork of the station buildings.

The station area is now occupied by the rear of the fire station and some small factory units, with nothing to denote that a station had ever stood on this site. *Hugh Ballantyne/RS*

RIPPLE was the next station south of Upton, and closed together with Upton in 1961. On 16 May 1957 0-6-0 No 43754, with 3rd Class brake carriage No M21026M, pauses with the 5.45pm Upton to Ashchurch service. By this time the near-side track was out of use.

Happily, today the station is well-restored and in private use. This 26 March 1999 photograph was taken by courtesy of the owner, Mrs Jeanette Young. *Hugh Ballantyne/RS*

70

Worcester Shrub Hill to Evesham and Honeybourne

SHRUB HILL (1): At around 8.00pm on 20 June 1983 Class 45 Type 4 diesel No 45036 enters Worcester Shrub Hill station past a splendid array of GWR-type semaphores, with the 1535 Leeds to Plymouth van train. At the rear of the train can be seen the remains of one of the two steam sheds, by then used as a stabling point for diesel locomotives and DMUs. On the left is the line to Foregate Street and Malvern.

On 21 May 1998 DMU No 158790 enters Shrub Hill with the 1030 Nottingham to Cardiff service. The shed buildings beyond the junction have gone, but the area is still a refuelling point, and happily the semaphore signals are still with us. *Both RS*

SHRUB HILL (2): Turning round from the previous scenes, we see ex-LMS Class '4F' 0-6-0 No 44516 waiting to depart from Shrub Hill with the 5.15pm Bristol-Birmingham New Street all-stations stopping train on 6 June 1959. These sturdy locomotives, introduced in 1922, were a Midland Railway design, equally at home on freight or passenger workings.

Today's picture shows that the '4F' of yesteryear has been replaced by 'Turbo' unit No 166216, leaving the station on the 1043 Paddington to Hereford service on 21 May 1998. A comparison with the 'past' picture shows that there are now only three tracks through the station. The old building on the left-hand side of the footbridge has gone, but some of the other buildings remain. *Michael Mensing/RS*

72

SHRUB HILL (3): The next two scenes at Shrub Hill were taken on the evening of 5 January 1984 and show Brush Type 4 diesel No 47482 waiting to leave platform 2 with the 1707 Paddington to Hereford train, and, at the other end of the station, 'Peak' No 45057 waiting for more parcels to be loaded on to a Leeds-Bristol van train before leaving for the south. *Both RS*

SHRUB HILL (4): On the very pleasant afternoon of 19 April 1987 Class 4 diesel No 47622, in the old blue livery, departs from Shrub Hill with the 1615 Hereford to Paddington train.

The equivalent view taken on 10 January 1998 shows ex-GWR 'King' Class 4-6-0 No 6024 *King Edward I* heading into the setting sun with a return special to Gloucester and Didcot, which outwards had run via Banbury and Birmingham to Worcester. The signal box and semaphore signals are still there, and on the right-hand side can be seen the roof of the old Midland Railway goods shed. Also, a comparison with the 1987 picture shows that some trackwork has gone. *Both RS*

The third picture was taken from near the far signal in the previous scenes, and shows Class 50 No 50031 *Hood* heading for Paddington with the 1615 train from Hereford on 9 April 1989. This area is known as the Midland yard (Shrub Hill being a joint GWR/LMS station), with Midland Railway architecture (the goods shed) being prominent on the left-hand side. *RS*

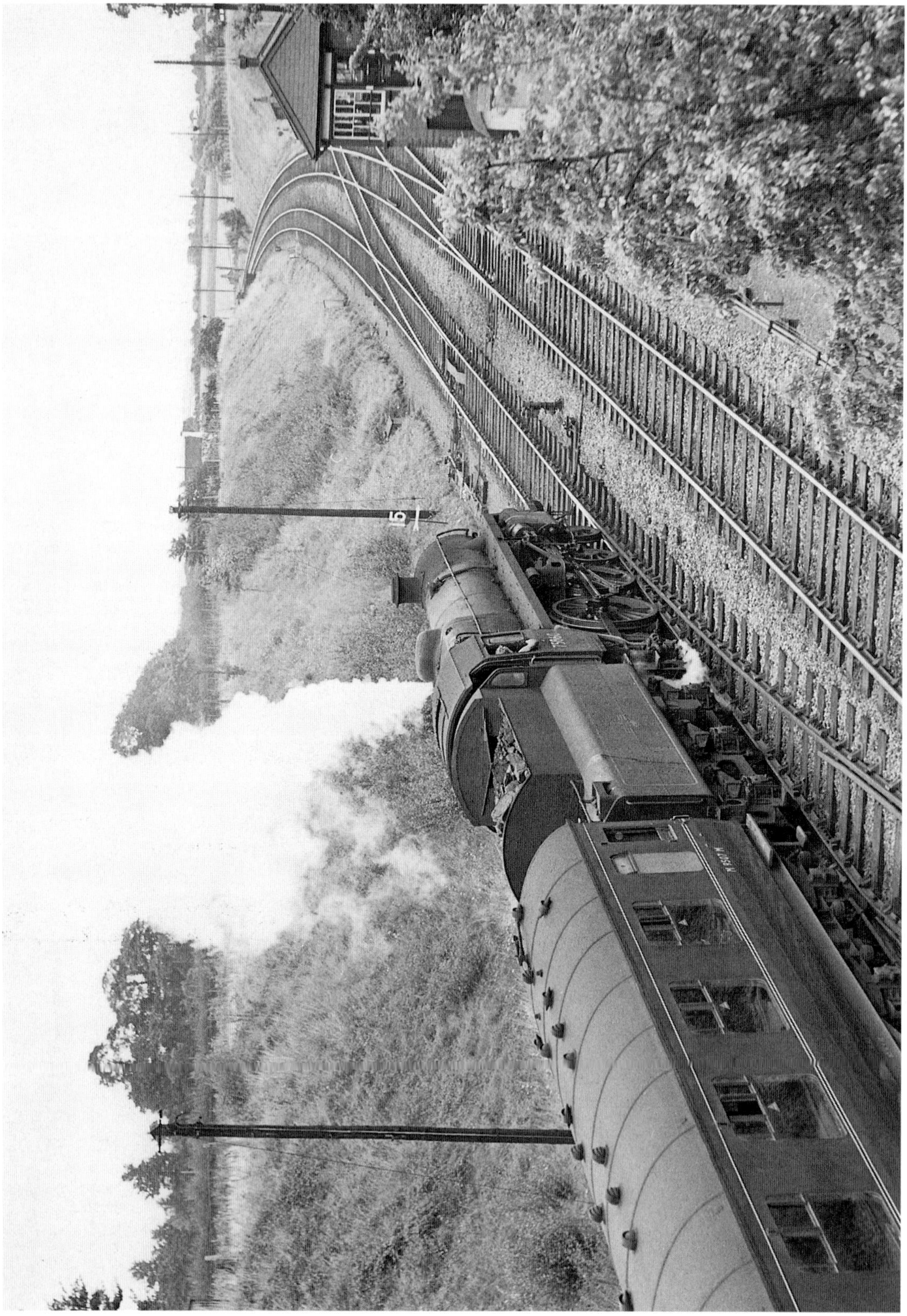

NORTON JUNCTION: Three miles south of Worcester Shrub Hill station is Norton Junction, where the line to Paddington and the line to Gloucester and Bristol part company. Just south of Norton Junction is Abbotswood Junction, where the Worcester line meets the main Birmingham to Bristol route, which has just passed under the Worcester-Paddington line (see the accompanying map). On 24 August 1963 Standard Class '4' 4-6-0 No 75060 heads through Norton Junction with the 2.44pm from Shrub Hill to Gloucester. The line to Paddington can be seen swinging away to the left. Behind the photographer is the site of the former Norton Junction Halt; this small station was for use mainly by the nearby barracks, and was closed in the 1960s. I well remember arriving here on New Year's Eve 1956 on a troop train from Harwich (we had left Germany the previous day); because of the shortness of the platforms it took us a considerable time to disembark.

Today the line to Paddington has been singled and the crossover for Worcester-bound trains from the Paddington line is situated a few yards behind the photographer near the site of the halt. 'Turbo' unit No 166202 heads for Worcester with the 1600 service from Oxford on 27 May 1998. *Michael Mensing/RS*

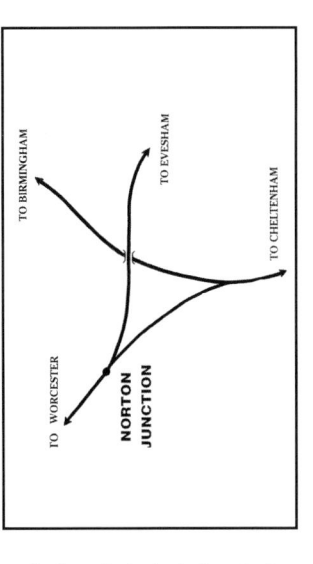

PERSHORE: Eight miles from Shrub Hill on the Paddington line is the delightful riverside town of Pershore, which, as can be seen in this early 1950s view, boasted a fine-looking GWR station, complete with impressive goods yard, goods shed and crane. This view is looking towards Oxford.

Except for the direction of the line and a few trees, nothing seems to remain of the 'past' view in today's equivalent, taken on 27 February 1999. Like many 19th-century stations, that at Pershore is sited a fair way from the town – about 1½ miles. *Joe Moss/RS*

78

EVESHAM (1): Six miles from Pershore and, like its smaller neighbour, set on the River Avon, Evesham is famous as a fruit and vegetable growing area, the whole district being known as the Vale of Evesham. Class 47 No 47231 has just crossed the River Avon to the north of Evesham and is about to enter the station with the diverted 0845 (Sundays only) Liverpool Lime Street to Paddington train on 25 September 1983. A northbound DMU is waiting for the token exchange to enable it to work the single line to Worcester.

The 'present' picture, taken on 27 January 1999, shows the rear of 'Turbo' unit No 165101 as it departs from Evesham with the 0948 Paddington to Hereford service. Some factory buildings have gone on either side of the line, but over the last 15/16 years very little has changed on the railway scene. *Both RS*

EVESHAM (2): In steam days there were two stations at Evesham – GWR and LMS – situated side-by-side, but when the LMS line, from Redditch to Evesham and on to Ashchurch, was closed in the 1960s, only the GWR station remained. On 9 May 1963 ex-LMS Class '8F' 2-8-0 No 48172 heads north-west through the station, passing 0-6-0 pannier tank No 3745 on shunting duties. To the right of the goods shed, out of sight, was the LMS or Midland station.

On 27 January 1999 DMU No 165101 pauses at Evesham with the 0948 Paddington to Hereford service. Relics of the past still remain, with the station still retaining its GWR canopies. *B. J. Ashworth/RS*

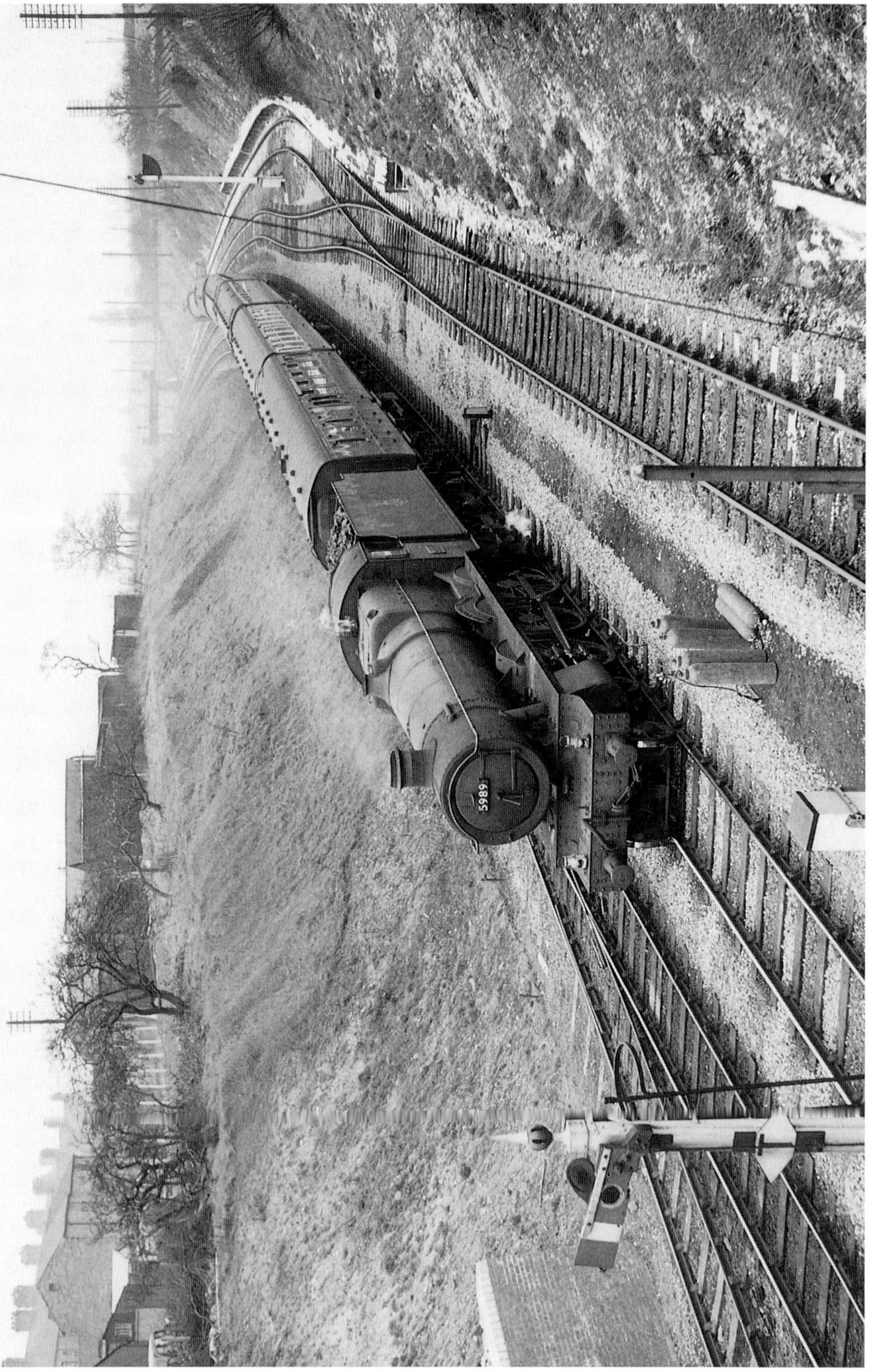
5989

EVESHAM (3): Ex-GWR 'Hall' Class 4-6-0 No 5989 *Cransley Hall* approaches Evesham (GWR) from the east with the 10.00am Paddington-Hereford train on 9 March 1958. To the east of Evesham the LMS and GWR lines roughly paralleled each other for about a quarter of a mile before the LMS line crossed the GWR and headed north. Beyond the rear of the train can be seen the bridge carrying the Redditch line over the Paddington route. Just beyond that bridge the GWR line once again crosses over the River Avon, the river forming a horseshoe around Evesham.

On 27 January 1999 the rear of Turbo unit No 166217 is seen in the same location forming the 1029 Worcester Foregate Street to Paddington service. The trackwork has been considerably modified, but the semaphore signals still remain. *Michael Mensing/RS*

EVESHAM (4): Looking back in the opposite direction, this picture clearly shows the position of the two stations, the LMS facility in the foreground. A connection between the two lines was made at the north-western end of the stations. On 14 April 1962 ex-LMS Class '4MT' 2-6-4T No 42416 pauses at Evesham Midland with the 4.30pm Ashchurch-Redditch service. Not many months after this picture was taken, in September 1962, the section from Evesham to Redditch was closed, then the Ashchurch-Evesham section closed in June the following year.

Today's view of the same location shows nothing of the remains of the old LMS station, but on 7 January 1999 the GWR station can be glimpsed in the centre of the picture. *Michael Mensing/RS*

HONEYBOURNE: Our final location on the Worcester-Paddington line is the famous junction station at Honeybourne; the junction itself is described in *British Railways Past and Present Special: Snow Hill to Cheltenham*. This 1930s scene shows a GWR '1400' Class 0-4-2 tank pausing at Honeybourne with an eastbound train, possibly to Kingham.

This station was later closed to passengers, but re-opened as a halt (using the old down main line platform) in 1981. On 1 April 1999, Turbo unit No 166204 speeds past the single platform with the 1248 Paddington to Great Malvern service. Some sidings still remain, as well as the remains of the up platform. *Lens of Sutton/RS*

Down the Lickey to Bromsgrove

BARNT GREEN (I): The former LMS main line from Birmingham to Bristol enters the county just over a mile north of Barnt Green, which is also the junction for the Redditch line. This view of Barnt Green, looking north towards Birmingham, was taken in August 1949 and shows the four-track section that ended here. On the right the Redditch lines run into their own platforms.

Today's view, taken on 23 May 1998, shows quite a few changes. The semaphore signals, sidings, small goods yard and goods platform have now gone, and the main line is only double track with a loop line. Also, the line from Birmingham New Street to Barnt Green and the branch line to Redditch are now 'under the wires', thus allowing an electrified cross-city commuter service between Redditch, Birmingham, Sutton Coldfield and Lichfield. *Joe Moss collection/RS*

REDDITCH is our next stop, on what was the loop line to Ashchurch. On 18 June 1960 ex-LMS Class '4MT' 2-6-2T No 42446 enters Redditch station with the empty stock for the 2.55pm to Evesham and Ashchurch. The line to Evesham/Ashchurch from Redditch closed in 1962, thus making Redditch the terminus of the line from New Street and Barnt Green.

Some years ago the old station was closed and rebuilt on the other side of the road bridge seen in the 'past' view, and there is now just a single track into the station with no run-round facilities. With electrification of the line in 1991, Redditch formed the southern terminal of the cross-city route from Lichfield, providing West Midlands commuters with a frequent service to and from Birmingham. This was the site of the old Redditch station on 28 March 1999, the road bridge identifying the location. *Michael Mensing/RS*

BARNT GREEN (2): We are now back on the Bristol main line at Barnt Green. This view, looking towards Bromsgrove, was taken in August 1949, just after nationalisation of the railways. By 20 March 1999 all the station buildings have gone and houses now occupy the fields on the right. *Joe Moss/RS*

90

BLACKWELL (1): Just over a mile south of Barnt Green, at the summit of the Lickey Bank (2 miles at 1 in 37¾ down to Bromsgrove) was Blackwell station. The next two 'past' pictures, taken in the early 1950s, show well the procedure used by banking engines. The first shows ex-LMS 'Black Five' 4-6-0 No 44966 running through the comparatively level section of track at Blackwell – the summit is just south of the station. The train is probably a Bristol-Birmingham service.

Today only in exceptional circumstances do trains require banking assistance. On 23 May 1998 Brush Type 4 No 47810 runs through Blackwell at the head of the 0755 Plymouth-Newcastle train. *Joe Moss/RS*

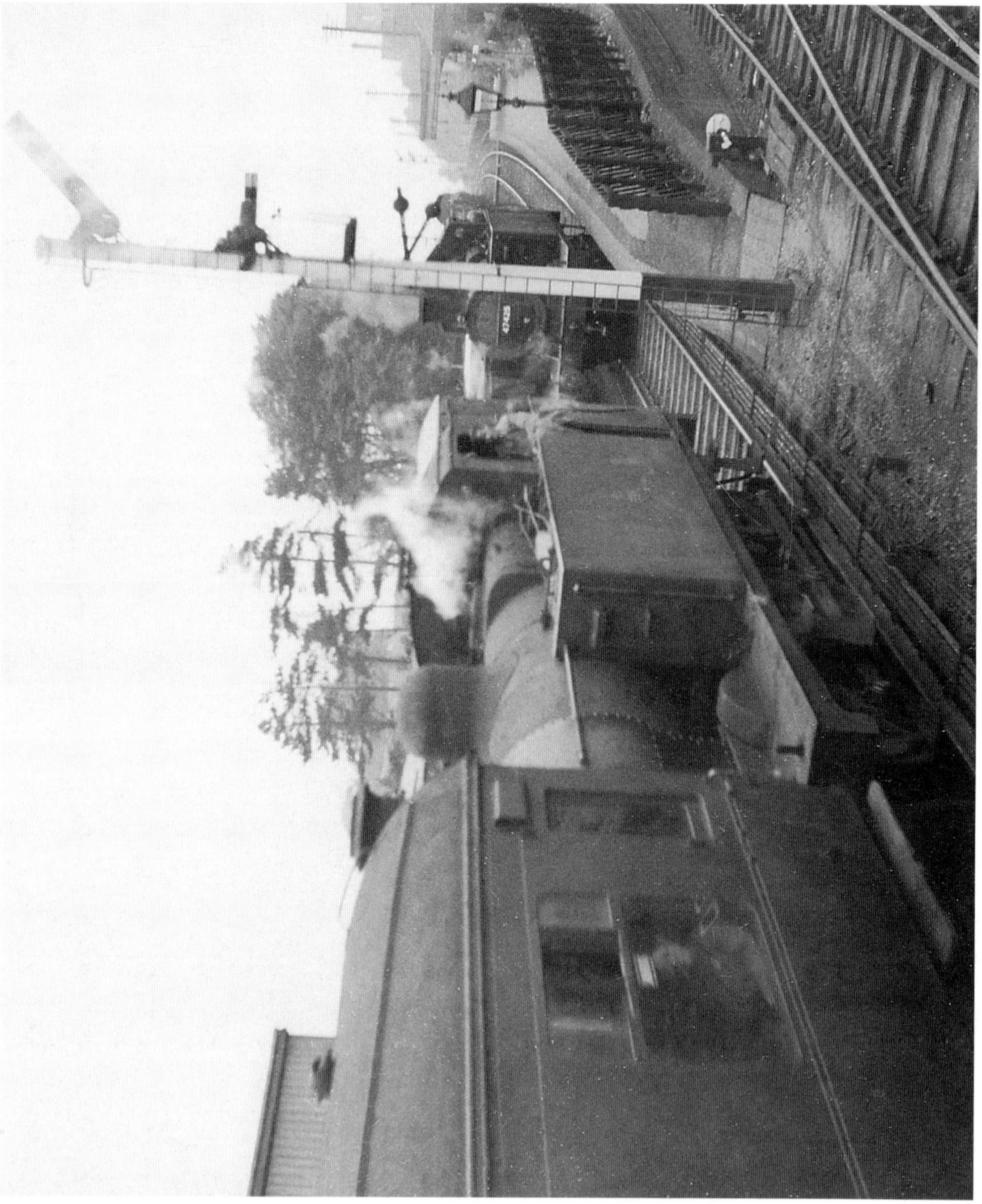

BLACKWELL (2): At the rear of the Bristol-Birmingham train are two ex-LMS 'Jinty' 0-6-0T banking engines (the second is No 47425), seen here leaving the train to return down the bank to Bromsgrove. Banking engines were not coupled up, thus saving a great deal of time. Note at the rear of No 47425 the top of the incline. These days very little is left of Blackwell station (it closed in 1964) except the station houses, just visible in the past picture. On the right of the last coach of the Plymouth-Newcastle train is the site of the old northbound platform, which made an ideal viewing point for the summit. *Joe Moss/RS*

94

LICKEY BANK (I): About half a mile south of Blackwell is Vigo Bridge, where the B4096 Lickey End to Tardebigge and Redditch road runs under the line, and at that point a public footpath crosses the line, making it an ideal place to observe trains on the Lickey Bank. In the early 1980s pairs of English Electric Class 37s were still used for banking duties, mainly on freight trains. They would normally be stabled at Worcester overnight, then spend the day at Bromsgrove being used as required. At 9.30am on 18 February 1983 Nos 37180 and 37270 make a fine sight in the winter sunshine as they bank a freight hauled by Class 25 No 25154 up to the summit at Blackwell. *Both RS*

LICKEY BANK (2): For many years the English Electric Class 50s worked passenger trains from the West Country to the north of England via Birmingham New Street. No 50006 *Neptune* powers up the bank, making an incredible sound, with the 1015 Bristol to Glasgow train on 17 February 1983. Note that although by this time it had been rebuilt, it was still in the old BR livery. *Neptune* was also one of the first of this famous class to be withdrawn, being taken out of service in July 1987. The entire class had been withdrawn by 1992, although happily many examples have been preserved privately, and are used on heritage lines as well as the main line. *RS*

This was the scene at Vigo Bridge on 23 May 1998, as a 156 unit heads up the bank with a Cardiff-Nottingham service. The imposing building seen in the earlier picture on page 95 has gone, to be replaced by a modern housing estate. *RS*

Above and above right LICKEY BANK (3): We are at Vigo Bridge again, this time on the west side of the line. On the evening of 20 April 1957 ex-LMS 'Jubilee' Class 4-6-0 No 45685 *Barfleur* makes a fine sight as it climbs up the Lickey with the 4.45pm Bristol to York train. It is banked by BR Standard Class '9F' 2-10-0 No 92079.

These days, because of the growth of lineside vegetation, photography from the west side at this location is not very practicable, as can be seen from this picture, taken on 23 May 1998, of HST No 43098 in charge of the 0715 Penzance to Edinburgh train. *Michael Mensing/RS*

Right We leave the Lickey Bank itself just south of Vigo Bridge, where the most famous of all the Lickey bankers, the Midland Railway 0-10-0 No 58100 – affectionately known to everyone as 'Big Bertha', probably after the First World War gun – banks a heavy freight train on 23 April 1949. The brake-van is also ex-Midland Railway stock. This attractive locomotive was designed by Fowler and introduced in 1919 specially for working on the Lickey Bank, and was withdrawn in May 1956. Over the years many locomotives were tried on banking duties, some more successful than others, but 'Big Bertha' remained top of the list. I well recall making several trips up the bank on Bristol to Birmingham trains in 1954, and remember the excitement and noise as we were banked away from Bromsgrove by No 58100. *F. W. Shuttleworth*

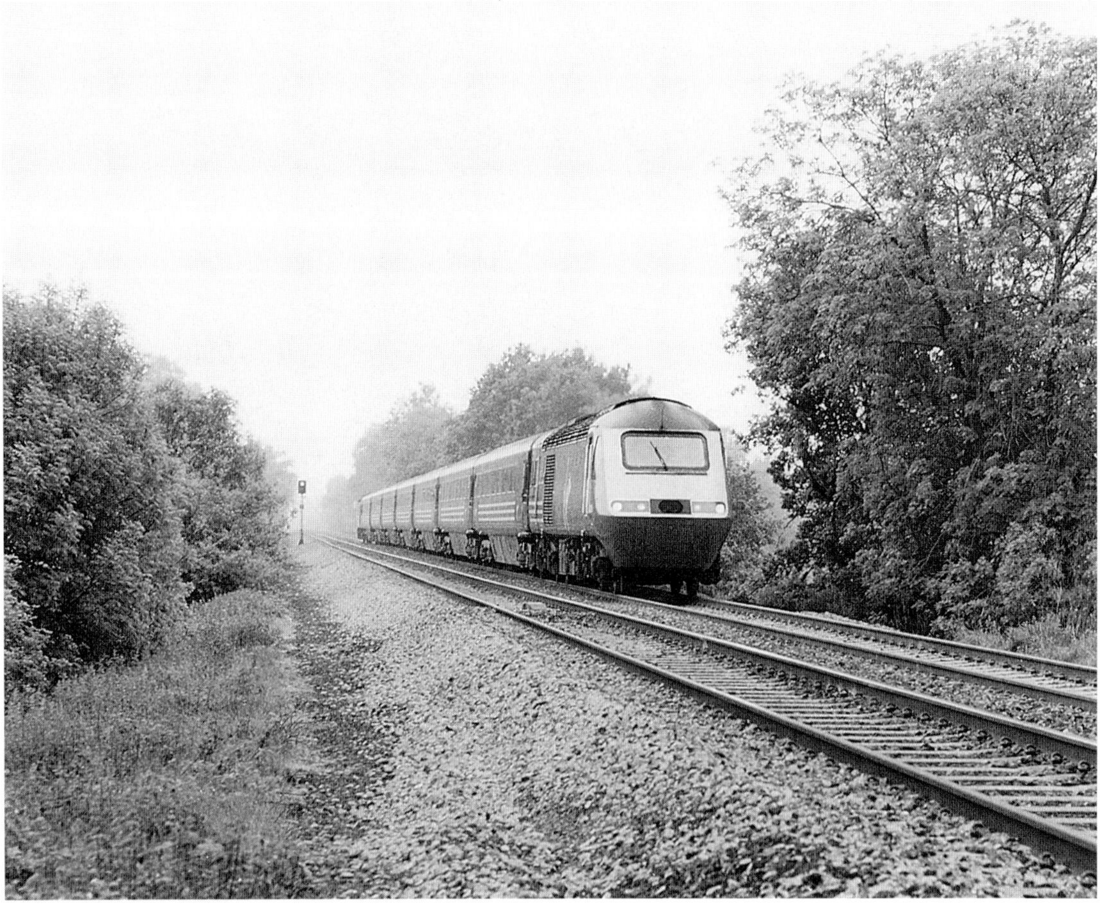

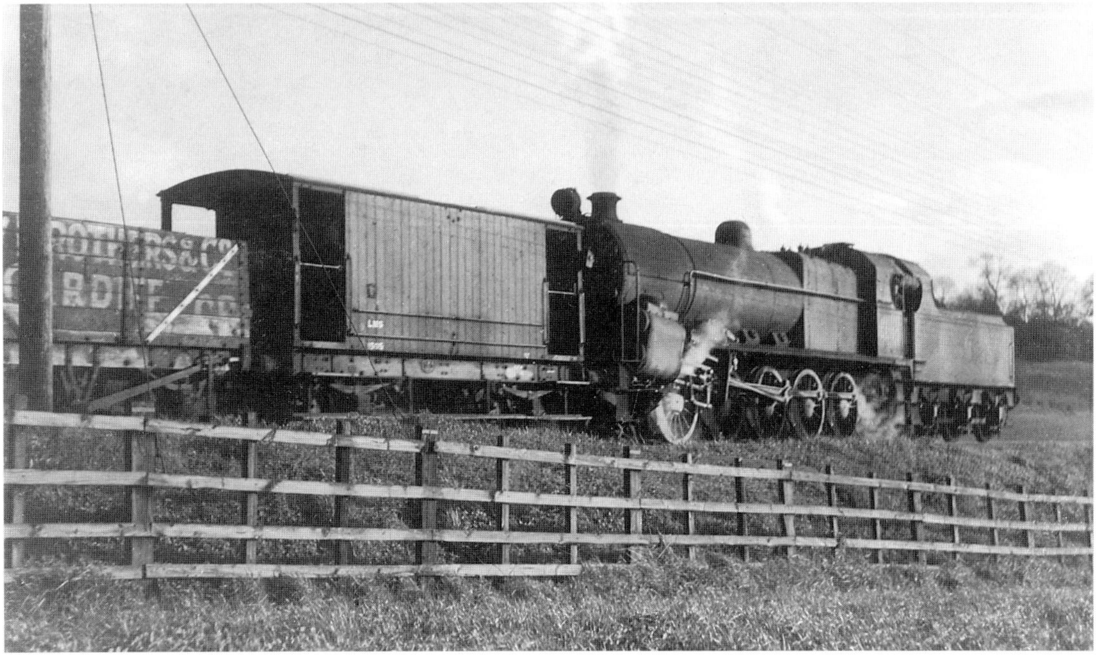

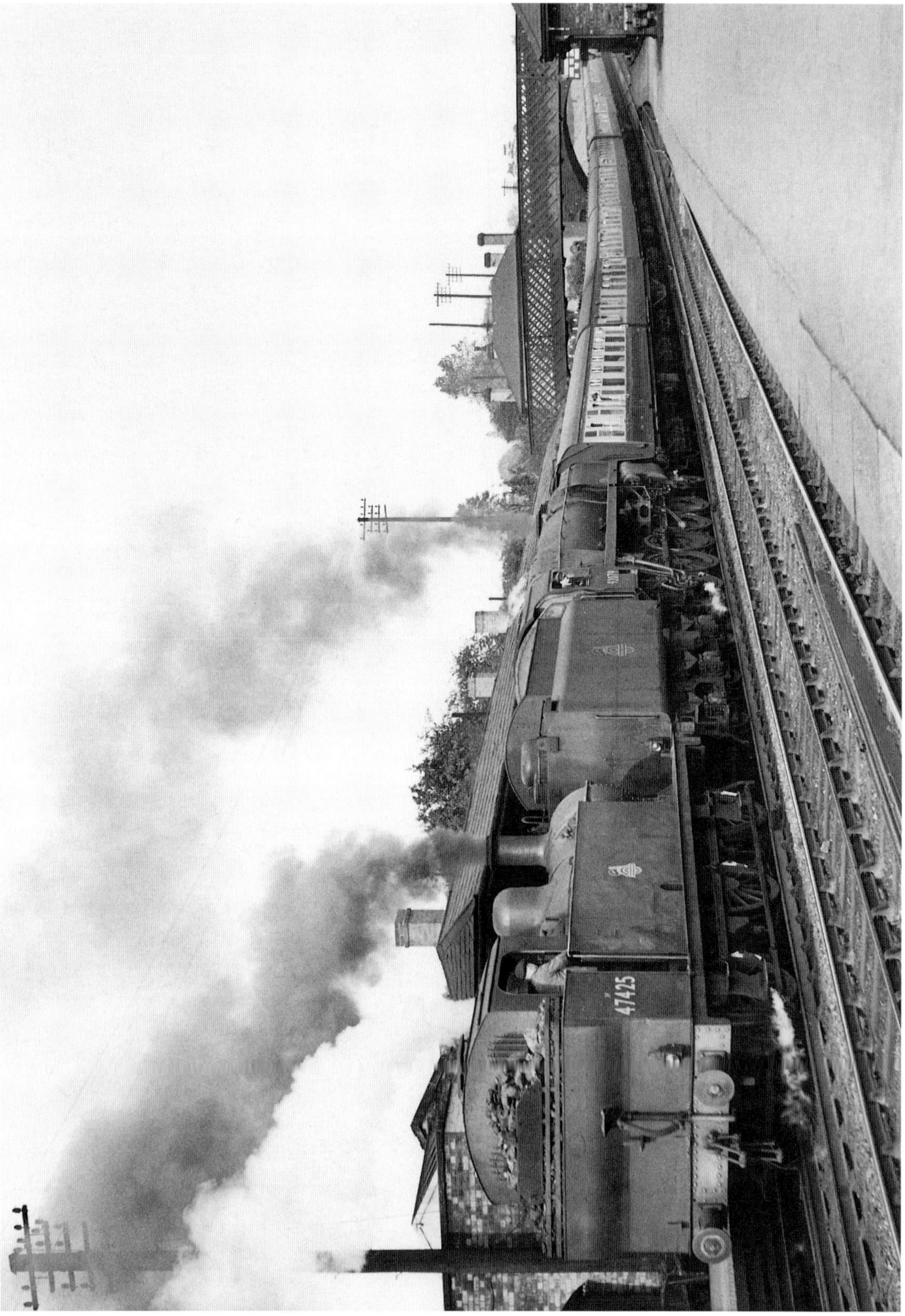
47425

BROMSGROVE (1): On 22 September 1956 BR Standard Class '9F' 2-10-0 No 92079 and ex-LMS Class '3F' 0-6-0T No 47425 bank a heavy passenger train out of Bromsgrove station. This picture well illustrates the steep gradient of the Lickey Bank. The '9F' took over from 'Big Bertha' when she was 'retired' in May 1956, having also been bequeathed the headlight from the famous 0-10-0.

Today the Lickey Bank remains, but the station has been modernised and now has only two tracks through it. On 23 May 1998 DMU No 156412 leaves the station and heads up the bank with the 1255 Cardiff to Nottingham service. *Michael Mensing/RS*

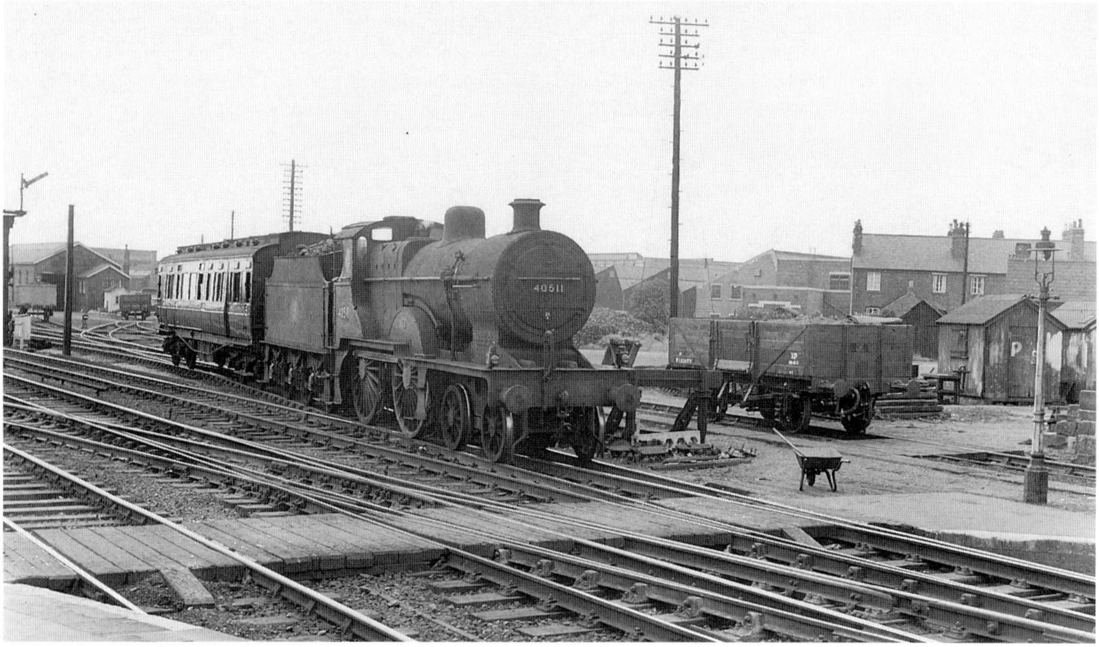
40511

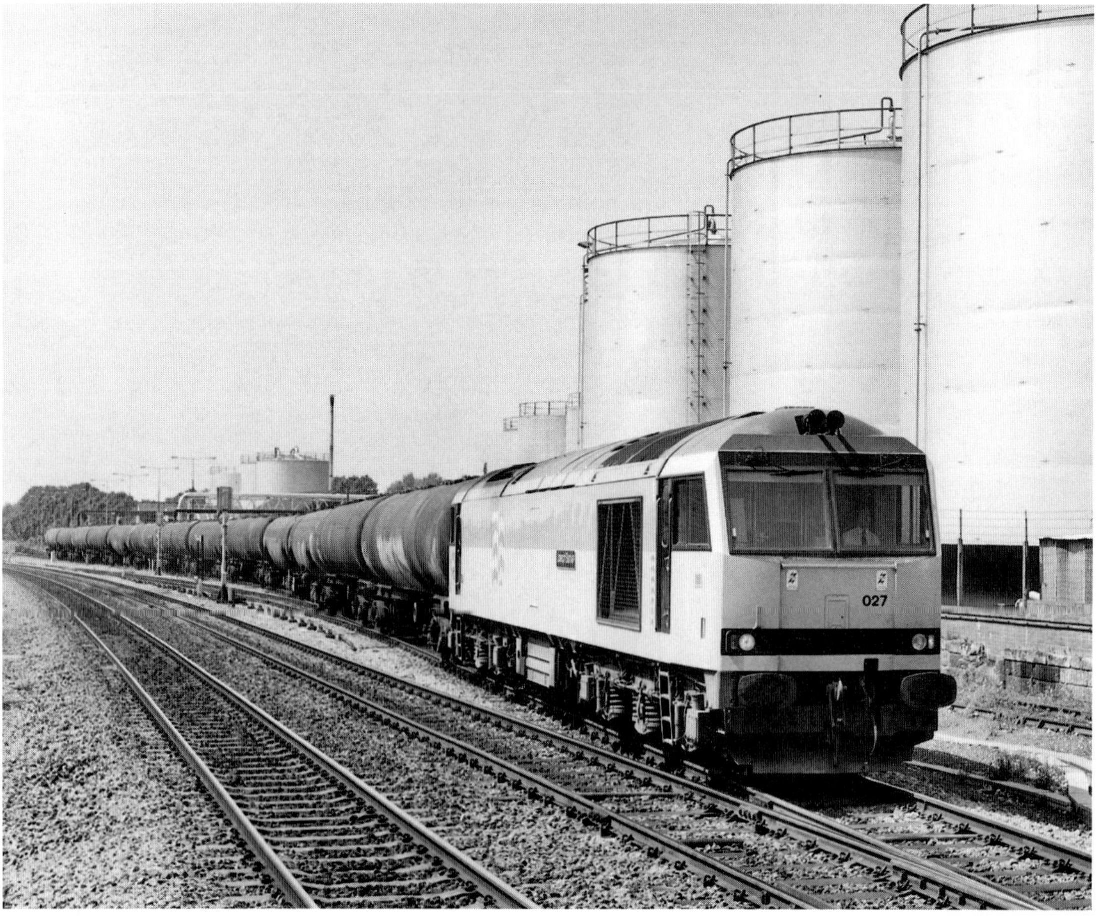
027

BROMSGROVE (2): On 11 September 1958 ex-LMS Class '2P' 4-4-0 No 40511 enters Bromsgrove station from the south with ex-Midland Railway inspection saloon No M932M. On the left can be seen the goods yard and Midland Railway goods shed.

The second photograph shows Class 60 diesel locomotive No 60027 leaving the sidings at the southern end of Bromsgrove station with a northbound tank train for Teesside on 20 June 1992.

The third of this trio of pictures was taken on 23 May 1998, and shows that the chemical tanks seen in the previous picture have gone completely, revealing once again the Midland goods shed, albeit minus the goods yard; the loop lines are still there but looking decidedly underused. Also, some of the houses seen in the 1958 picture survive. *F. W. Shuttleworth/RS (2)*

BROMSGROVE SHED: The shed, which closed in 1964, was situated on the eastern side of the station at its southern end. Its main function was to house the banking locomotives used on the Lickey Incline. The first picture of the shed was taken on 5 July 1959, and shows on the left an ex-GWR Class '9400' 0-6-0 pannier tank, and on the right ex-LMS Class '3F' 0-6-0T No 47276.

The next scene shows ex-LNER 2-8-8-2 articulated Garratt locomotive No 69999 at Bromsgrove shed on 23 April 1949. This Garratt, together with other large engines tried on the bank, including ex-LNWR 0-8-4 tank No 7953 in 1929-30 and LMS Beyer Garratt No 47998 in 1934, were all largely unsuccessful and could never match 0-10-0 No 58100 'Big Bertha'.

The third view of 'Big Bertha' banking a northbound passenger train was taken just south of the station in the early 1920s, during Midland Railway days. After her retirement in 1956, BR Standard Class '9F' 2-10-0 No 92079 took over the main banking duties, and was generally regarded as being a successful replacement with, of course, help from the ex-GWR and LMS 0-6-0 tanks.

The final scene shows the site of the shed on 23 May 1998. Beyond the embankment where the shed was sited is now a housing estate. *R. S. Carpenter collection/F. W. Shuttleworth/Lens of Sutton/RS*

105

Bromsgrove to Ashchurch

SOUTH OF BROMSGROVE: Almost half a mile south of Bromsgrove station Type 4 'Peak' Class diesel No D15 hurries past with the down 'Devonian', the Bradford to Paignton train, on 24 February 1962. The banking engines wait in the sidings for their next turn of duty; visible are '9F' No 92079 and pannier tanks Nos 8480 and 8402.

The present-day scene dates from 23 May 1998, with an HST set forming the 'Cornish Scot' from Edinburgh to Penzance speeding past the same location. Some of the sidings are now gone, as are the signal box and semaphore signals.

The third view is an earlier telephoto picture taken on 15 May 1992 on the other side of the line. We can again see the chemical tanks that have since been removed and the new housing estate, part of which is on the old locomotive shed site. On the right can just be seen the edge of the old turntable well. The time is 1825 and the southbound mixed goods is hauled by English Electric Class 37 No 37711 in light grey livery. *Michael Mensing/RS (2)*

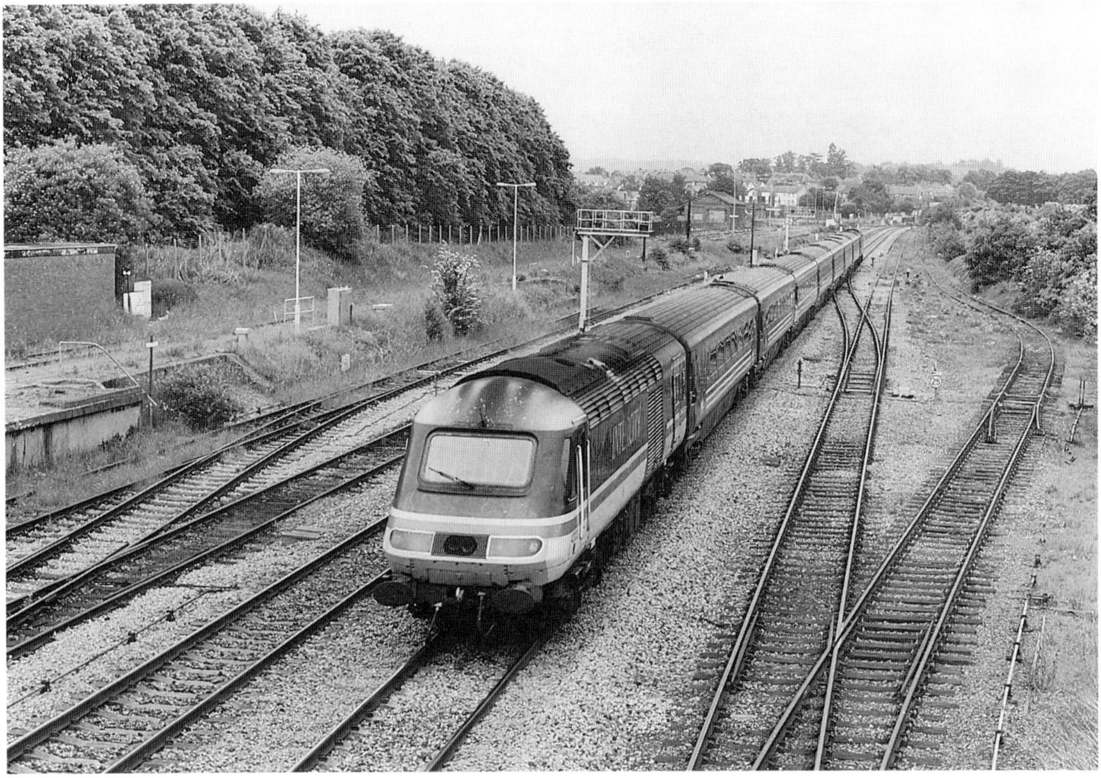

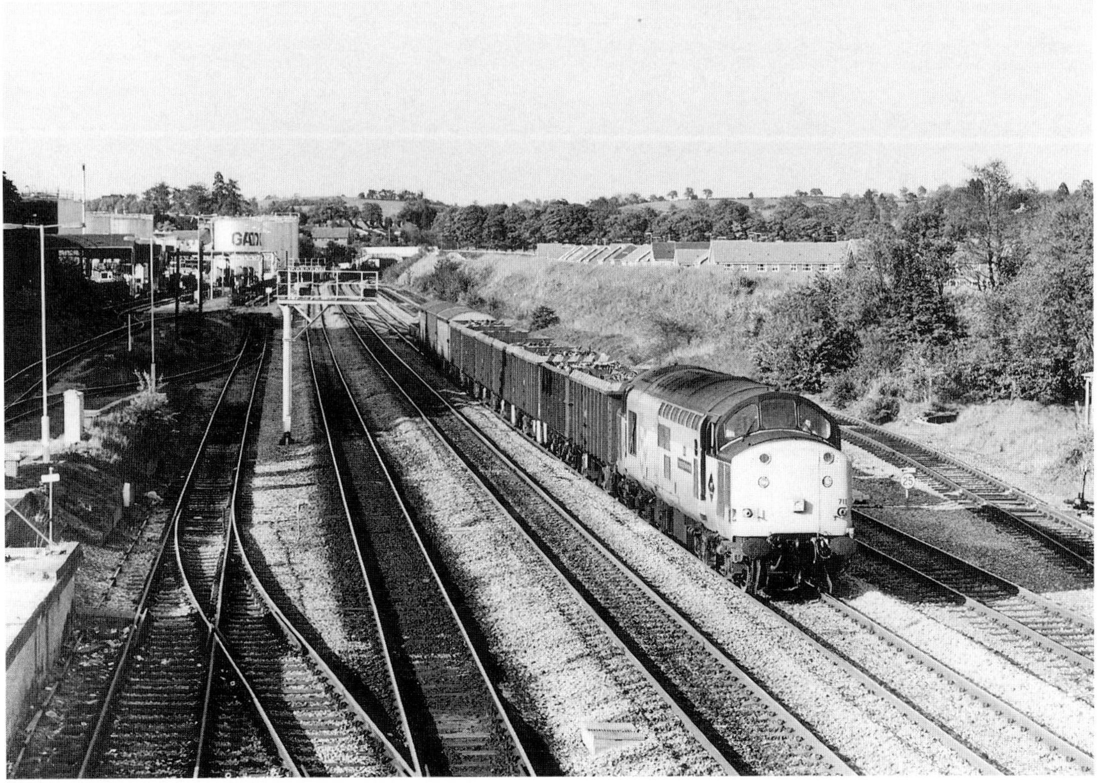

NEAR DROITWICH ROAD GOODS: Just over 2 miles south of Bromsgrove, at Stoke Works Junction, the main Birmingham-Bristol line and the Droitwich/Worcester loop line diverge, to rejoin at Abbotswood Junction (see the map on page 77) some 11 miles further south. On 3 May 1963 BR Standard Class '9F' 2-10-0 No 92138 is seen halfway along this 11-mile section with a heavy southbound coal train. The location is south of Droitwich Road goods station.

At roughly the same location today the 1629 New Street to Bristol HST hurries past on 24 May 1998. Because of the growth of trees and bushes, it was impossible to photograph at the same angle as the 'past' picture. *Michael Mensing/RS*

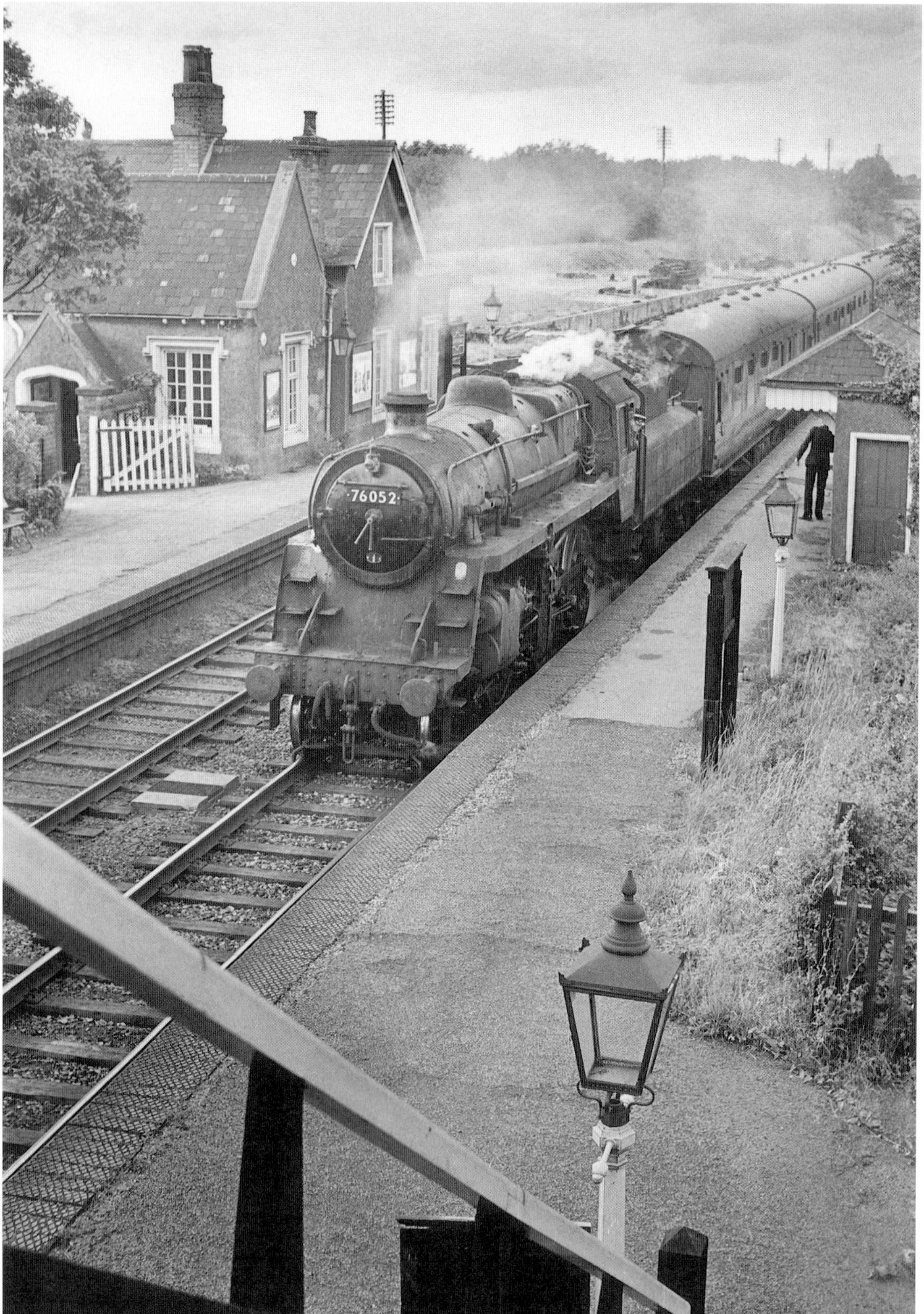
76052

DEFFORD: On 18 August 1964 BR Standard Class '4' 2-6-0 No 76052 runs smoothly into the picturesque station at Defford with a Worcester-Bristol stopping train.

The second photograph, taken in the early 1950s, shows that Defford was also convenient for Pershore, which is just over 2 miles north-west of Defford station.

The final picture was taken at the site of Defford station on 4 November 1995 and shows ex-GWR '73XX' Class 2-6-0 No 7335 with a Stourbridge Junction to Bristol charter train. The station was closed in the 1960s and only the surrounding landscape provides a link with the past. *B. J. Ashworth/Lens of Sutton/RS*

Also at Defford, but looking south, we see 'Peak' Class diesel No 45059 with the 1132 Penzance-New Street-Manchester train on 20 July 1985. Dominating the background is Bredon Hill. *RS*

ECKINGTON: Just over a mile south of Defford is the attractive village of Eckington, which until the 1960s boasted a smart-looking station. This view of the station, looking towards Birmingham, was taken between 1951 and 1953.

In contrast, on 27 May 1998 black-liveried Class 47 No 47712 approaches the site of the station, which closed in 1965, with the 1225 Stafford-Bristol train. The level crossing has now gone, replaced by a bridge for pedestrians only. Access to either side of the village is gained by the road bridge just discernible at the rear of the train. *Joe Moss/Christina Siviter*

BREDON is our final Worcestershire location on the Birmingham-Bristol main line, and this view was also taken between 1951 and 1953 facing Birmingham.

Today's view shows that although the station has long been closed, the station house is now privately owned, and the small waiting room on the up platform looks as if it is still used as a store. Bredon is 22 miles south of Bromsgrove and 2 miles north of Ashchurch. *Joe Moss/RS*

ASHCHURCH (1): Although Ashchurch is on the northern borders of Gloucestershire, I have included it here to round off the book. On 6 June 1959 Class '3F' 0-6-0 No 43210 (a Midland Railway design) heads north through Ashchurch with an evening mixed goods. This lovely old station was the junction for Tewkesbury and Upton-on-Severn (originally Great Malvern) to the north-west, and Evesham and Redditch to the north-east. Both lines converged at the southern end of the station and each had its own platform, curving away from those on the main line.

Ashchurch station was closed in the 1960s but was rebuilt on the same site and re-opened in 1995, now known as Ashchurch for Tewkesbury. On 27 May 1998 unit No 158822 enters Ashchurch with the 0916 Swansea to Birmingham New Street service. The only points of identification with the 1959 picture are the road bridge that carries the Tewkesbury to Evesham road, and the conifer tree on the left. *Michael Mensing/RS*

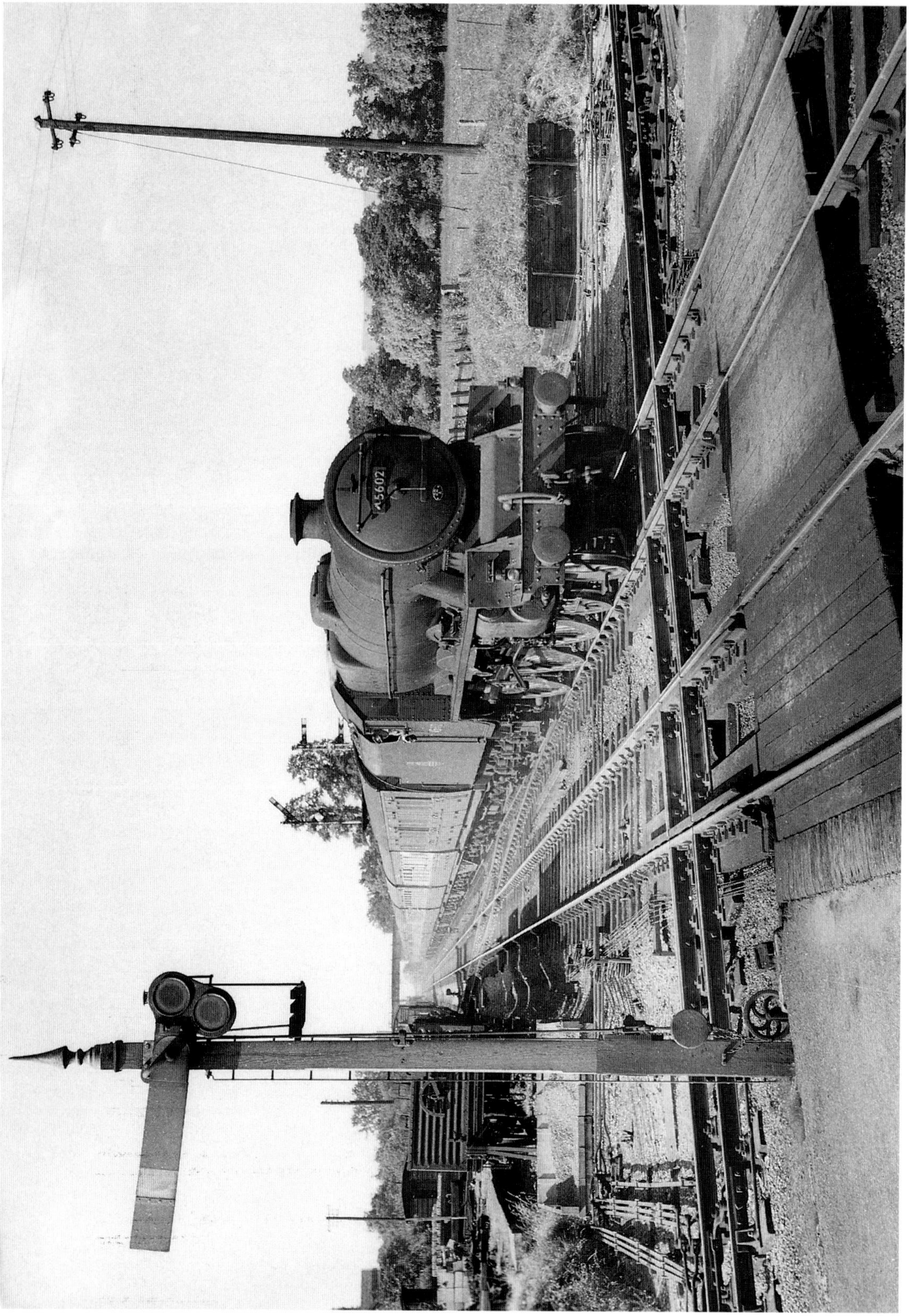

ASHCHURCH (2): On 9 July 1955 ex-LMS 'Jubilee' Class 4-6-0 No 45602 *British Honduras* (shedded at 22A Bristol) speeds over the line that linked the Tewkesbury and Evesham lines at the northern end of Ashchurch station (to enable through running) with the 12.30pm York to Bristol express. (See the accompanying map, which shows the junction layout.) Note the lovely Midland starter signal.

Today Ashchurch is a junction station no longer, as can be seen by this picture of a Class 47 diesel as it heads south at the same location with a midday passenger train on 25 May 1998. *Hugh Ballantyne/RS*

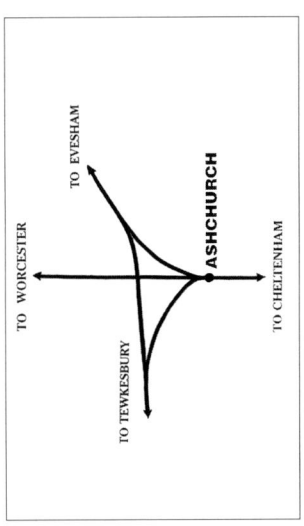

117

ASHCHURCH (3): This view of the station on 29 July 1961 shows ex-LMS Class '4MT' 2-6-4T No 42419 in the Evesham/Redditch platform. Having brought in the 5.00pm service from Birmingham New Street to Redditch and Ashchurch, it is just pulling out the empty stock to be stored in the adjacent siding. The line to Tewkesbury (and its platform) can be seen on the right-hand side of the main-line platform, beyond which is a goods platform.

Today all that remains of the Evesham line is a short spur to a local works – the new style of footbridge has obliterated the rest of the view on 27 May 1998. The Evesham/Redditch line and the Tewkesbury/Upton-on-Severn lines were closed in the 1960s. *Michael Mensing/RS*

118

ASHCHURCH (4): These two pictures show a modern past and present! As recently as 11 April 1994 an unidentified Class 47 with a midday southbound parcels train speeds through the empty site of Ashchurch station. Just four years later, on 27 May 1998, DMU No 158824 pulls out of the new station with the 1043 Birmingham New Street to Cardiff service. *Both RS*

Special trains in Worcestershire

Over the past years many steam and diesel specials have been run throughout the county, and the first of this small selection of photographs, taken on 3 September 1985, depicts ex-GWR 4-4-0 No 3440 *City of Truro* heading north up the Bristol-Birmingham main line near Defford with a return Gloucester to Worcester test run. *RS*

'Britannia' 'Pacific' No 70000 *Britannia* comes off the Gloucester line at Norton Junction with a Didcot-Gloucester-Worcester charter train on 25 July 1993. *RS*

With the first steam passenger train up the Lickey Bank for more than 30 years, ex-LMS 'Mogul' No 2968 and ex-GWR 2-6-0 No 7325 climb the notorious incline on 22 November 1997 with a Bristol-Birmingham-Walsall special. *RS*

Former GWR 'Castle' Class 4-6-0 No 5029 *Nunney Castle* crosses the canal just east of Worcester Foregate Street station with a Didcot to Great Malvern train on 8 June 1991. *RS*

123

Reviving memories of BR steam days, *Nunney Castle* heads out of Worcester for Oxford with the 'Cathedrals Express' on 27 June 1993. In the 1950s and early 1960s this named express was the number one passenger train between Paddington, Worcester and Hereford, and was usually hauled by one of the famous 'Castle' Class locomotives. *RS*

An illustrious visitor to Worcestershire on 13 April 1997 was English Electric 'Deltic' No D9000 *Royal Scots Grey*, seen here passing the site of Defford station with a Euston-New Street-Bristol-Paddington train. *RS*

On 14 April 1984 a series of football specials were run from Plymouth to Witton for Villa Park, where Plymouth Argyle were involved in the FA Cup semi-final. Some ran via the Lickey route and some via Stourbridge Junction. One of the return specials (via Stourbridge Junction) is seen here at Langley Green, hauled by Class 50 No 50033 *Glorious*. *RS*

The English Electric Class 50 locomotives could be seen daily in Worcestershire for many years, either on the Bristol-Birmingham main line or on Paddington-Worcester-Hereford trains. After their withdrawal from service many were preserved, including *Glorious*, and on 4 April 1992 she is joined by D400 (the original number of 50050 *Fearless*) as they head downhill at Stoke Prior, south of Bromsgrove, with a Derby to South Wales special charter train. *RS*

INDEX OF LOCATIONS

Ashchurch 115-119

Barnt Green 86-87, 89
Bewdley 48-49
Blackwell 90-93
Blakedown 45-46
Blowers Green 30-31
Bredon 114
Brettell Lane 26
Brierley Hill (Round Oak steel works) 27
Bromsgrove 100-107, 127
    shed 104-105

Cradley Heath 20

Defford 110-112, 120, 125
Droitwich 53
Droitwich Road Goods (near) 108-109
Dudley 32

Eckington 113

Evesham 8, 79-84

Great Malvern 64-65

Hagley 42-44
Halesowen 14-16
Hartlebury 52
Honeybourne 85

Kidderminster 47

Langley Green 9, 126
Lickey Bank 6, 94-99, 122
Lyde Green 21-23

Malvern Link 63
Malvern Wells 66-67

Netherton (near) 28-29
Norton Junction 76-77, 121

Old Hill 12-13, 18-19
    Tunnel 10-11

Pershore 78

Redditch 88
Ripple 69
Rubery 17

Severn Valley Railway 50-51
Stourbridge Junction 33-35, 37-41
    shed 24-25
Stourbridge Town 36
Suckley 62

Upton-on-Severn 68

Worcester Foregate Street 58-59, 123
    Rainbow Hill Tunnel 54-55
    Severn Bridge 60-61
    Shrub Hill 70-75, 124
    Tunnel Junction 56-57